ALASTAIR & SARAH
JONES

KT-493-328

CHRISTIAN YOUTH WORK

Christian Youth Work

MARK ASHTON

KINGSWAY PUBLICATIONS
EASTBOURNE

Copyright © Mark Ashton 1986

First published 1986
Reprinted 1987

All rights reserved.
No part of this publication may be reproduced or
transmitted in any form or by any means, electronic
or mechanical, including photocopy, recording, or any
information storage and retrieval system, without
permission in writing from the publisher.

ISBN 0 86065 428 1

Unless otherwise indicated, biblical quotations are from the
Revised Standard Version, copyrighted 1946, 1952,
© 1971, 1973 by the Division of Christian Education
of the National Council of the Churches of
Christ in the USA

Cover design by Drummond Chapman

**For Fiona,
my companion in youth work as in everything else**

Printed in Great Britain for
KINGSWAY PUBLICATIONS LTD
Lottbridge Drove, Eastbourne, E. Sussex BN23 6NT by
Richard Clay Ltd, Bungay, Suffolk
Typeset by CST, Eastbourne

Contents

Acknowledgements

As I look back over the five years that I have worked towards this book, I realize that the list of acknowledgements could be almost unending. Every youth worker with whom I have spoken and nearly every book which I have read have shaped my thinking. However, conversations and correspondence with a number of individuals made a special contribution: Alan Dodds, Bob Moffett, Leslie Francis, John Pridmore, Tony Campolo, Pauline Bell, David Blair, Tony Porter, Lance Pierson, Michael Eastman, Graham Cray, Anton Baumohl, Ken Wycherley, Don Humphries, the late Jim Punton, Dave Roberts, Gavin Reid, Garth Hewitt, Nick McKinnel, Clive Calver, Steve Wilcockson, Colin Matthews, Sue Howard and Cathy Smith—all these sowed ideas in my mind that have come to fruition in this book. Not all its conclusions will be to their liking, but for their help I am grateful.

A number of friends read early drafts and I benefited greatly from their comments: Lester Barr, John Hamilton, Jonathan Fletcher, Graham Tomlin, Colin Fletcher, David Day, Tony Perry, Jeremy Taylor, Rob Musgrave, Arthur McBryan, John Allan, Henry Corbett, June Hughman, John

Chapman, Jimmy Oratayo, Hugh Palmer, and, very especially, Christopher Byworth.

To my colleagues in the youth department of CPAS I owe a debt of gratitude, particularly the late Richard Bowdler, Clive Grinham, and John Simmons. Heather Linnecar provided invaluable administrative and research assistance. Stevie Beljung showed immense diligence and patience in typing and retyping the manuscript.

This book would never have been possible without the giving by countless churches to the Church Pastoral Aid Society, which is the parent organization of CYFA (the Church Youth Fellowships Association), my employer for the last five years.

Introduction

In the autumn of 1981 I started a new job with great reluctance. It was not because I had to move my family from a pleasant county town to the city that I was downhearted. It was the prospect of the job itself.

I was being employed by a national organization to help the work of the local church with older teenagers. One glance told me that this was an area of frightening weakness. In so many churches the older teenagers are the scarcest members of the congregation. I could see a few encouraging signs of life, but the overwhelming impression was that Christians had not thought out their approach to teenagers.

Where thought had been given to the matter, it seemed to be on shaky foundations. One national youth officer has written: 'Adolescence is a recognized contemporary phenomenon and the tools for understanding it are secular ones.' While I understand what lies behind that remark, I have come to believe that it is profoundly mistaken. Christians have subconsciously assumed that the Bible has little to teach us about young people growing up at the end of the twentieth century. The weakness of Christian youth work today is a result.

Christian youth work must be distinct in its aim (because Christians have a unique view of what it is to be a human being), and also distinct in its methods (because God has not left us at the mercy of contemporary fashions in the social sciences, but has provided us with guidelines for understanding adolescence in our own particular culture).

I am not an academic theologian and this book is not a systematic theology of youth. Neither is it a practical handbook of church youth work. But it is concerned with theory and it is concerned with theology. It is written out of a great desire to give Christians a renewed vision for young people, a new confidence in what they can do for them, how they can do it, and why they should do it.

I have tried not to tell the stories of my friends. There have been a number of good books published telling stories of youth work. My approach is theoretical rather than anecdotal. Obviously I have referred in passing to my own experiences with young people, but I do not think that 'my experience' in itself should be accorded any authority. The most important test is not that the ideas in this book work in practice (which they do), but that they come from, and are true to, the Bible.

I have followed one practice that some readers may find irritating. When writing about youth leaders and young people, I have deliberately switched genders regularly. It seemed the only way to avoid giving the impression that youth ministry is reserved for one sex or the other. It may be disconcerting, but it does make a valuable point.

I do not believe that the years from thirteen to twenty have a special value above that of other ages, but they are significant for the personal development of the individual. In young people we see a microcosm of society and, very often, a thermometer of the health of the church. Much of what I have written applies to adults as well as to teenagers. It is not my task to make that application, but I am well aware how wide the discussion could become at some points.

This is not a book for young people. It is a book for concerned adults about young people and the church. The church is the body of Christ. Whether we like the idea or not, the church (in all its forms and failures) is where Jesus is in the world today. He has a heart for the young. So must we, if we would be faithful to him, and if we would fulfil his commission to the young people of our day.

I

The Young Own the Town
Adolescence in late twentieth-century Western society (i)

The teenage phenomenon

Someone has suggested that teenagers 'were born in 1942, marketed in America in 1947, discovered in small flocks in Britain in 1956, cosseted and comforted during the 1960s, began to weaken as youth unemployment climbed in the 1970s, and can now be pronounced extinct'. It was in 1951 that Alan Freed, a radio disc jockey in Cleveland, Ohio, apparently first used the term 'rock 'n roll' to describe the music he was playing. The word 'teenager' itself was only coined during the Second World War by market researchers who wanted to describe young people with money to spend. Some sociologists are now suggesting they were a phenomenon unique to a period of affluence which has come to an end.

Certainly something happened to British society in the years following the Second World War which gave a new prominence to young people.[1] By the late 1950s young people were much richer than they had ever been before. Their spending power was a new development in the national economy, which did not go unnoticed for long.[2]

While there were other significant factors, like the ending of National Service, the explosion of youth culture in the early 1960s can be explained in terms of this new young spending power. The Beatles and the Rolling Stones were not necessarily playing better music than any of their predecessors, nor was David Bailey a better photographer, nor Jean Shrimpton a more attractive model, nor was Mary Quant designing better clothes. It was simply that the economic tide was right for them. The pop culture of the 1960s was largely created by the affluence of the 'you've-never-had-it-so-good' years that followed 1945.

This youth market (now estimated at £2,000 million) is still an important factor, even though the rapid economic growth of the 1960s has declined. The young continue to attract much commercial attention, because they can easily be exploited by advertising (the advertising industry's skill in manipulating images gives it a powerful hold over the image-conscious adolescent's aspiration to adulthood).

We are 'youth conscious' in Britain today. Almost every successful product has to be given a 'young' image by media advertising. Old age is not popular. By focusing public attention on youth-related problems, like inner-city riots, and on the more extreme manifestations of youth culture, like punk hairstyles, the media have provided a new dimension to the public's consciousness of the centuries-old problem of the generation gap. We are being encouraged to think that there is something special and different about the young, to view them as a group, a peculiar social category.

These are recent developments. To some extent their origin is economic. But there are other factors as well. For example, the contemporary idolatry of youth is only one side of a coin. The other side is a fear of old age and a shunning of death throughout our society, which cannot be explained in economic terms.

So we will need to go further back than the 1950s and 1960s to understand how we arrived at where we are today.

A glance at history

> Youth has no regard for old age, and the wisdom of the centuries is looked down upon both as stupidity and foolishness. The young men are indolent; the young women are indecent and indecorous in their speech, behaviour and dress.

That was written eight centuries ago, by Peter the Hermit in 1114. Whenever the 'teenager' may have emerged, the young have been seen as a problem throughout history. In the middle of the fourth century B.C. Aristotle wrote, 'When I look at the younger generation, I despair for the future of civilization!'

The actual limits of youth have been variously defined down the centuries. For the Romans 'adolescence' covered a period from seventeen to about twenty-eight. In the Middle Ages, youth lasted from the end of dependence at seven or eight to the achievement of independence and marriage in the mid- to late-twenties. It was the Industrial Revolution that shaped our present understanding of the end of childhood and the beginning of manhood or womanhood.

The Factory Acts of 1833 and 1847 protected young people between thirteen and eighteen from the full rigours of factory life, and the Youthful Offenders Act of 1834 distinguished young from adult criminals. The wealth created by industrialization allowed the development of private education. Once boarding-school education became fashionable among the middle classes after the 1830s the age of thirteen assumed a new significance. This made a distinction between primary and secondary education which fixed a lower limit for adolescence. It was in the nineteenth century that special books and magazines for the young began to appear (*Tom Brown's Schooldays* was published in 1857 and *The Boys' Own Paper* first appeared in 1879).

The nineteenth century also saw the beginnings of state education. In 1833 the government voted £20,000 to be divided equally between the established and the non-conformist churches in order to set up schools. (This did not compare particularly favourably with the £50,000 they voted to the Royal Stables at Windsor!) In 1839 another £30,000 was voted and a special Education Committee was set up. There were still no state-paid teachers or inspectors. By the middle of the century, the annual parliamentary grant had risen to £500,000, but it was not until 1870 that a system of local School Boards was established by the Forster Education Act. This laid the foundation for a state system of education.

By 1880 there were enough schools for attendance to be made compulsory up to the age of ten. This was raised to twelve in 1899, fourteen in 1918 and sixteen in 1972.

Over the last century and a half adolescence has been democratized.The abolition of child labour, the introduction of education for all, the progressive raising of the school-leaving age, and the setting up of institutions like Juvenile Courts have all ensured that everyone is now guaranteed an official period of youth. There is a special time between being a child and being an adult, a moratorium for adjustment and development granted to everyone who grows up in the West.

Health and diet

But the industrial wealth of the Western World has had less obvious consequences for growing up. Better health care and better nutrition have meant that people in the West have grown larger and matured earlier than ever before. Today's average six-year-old is about twelve centimetres taller than a child of the same age at the turn of the century. In Norway in 1850 the average age at which teenage girls first experienced menstruation was seventeen years. By 1950 it was thirteen years. Today in Britain one girl in four begins menstruating at primary school. An improvement in diet—especially during infancy—is the most plausible explanation currently available as to why we reach maturity earlier now than we did a hundred years ago.

At whatever age society may choose to accord adult status

to a child, his or her body is according it earlier and earlier. We now have young people who are sexually mature long before they will be treated as adults by the community in which they are growing up.

There is a significant difference between boys and girls here. Girls commonly mature about two years earlier than boys. They undergo more obvious changes. Menstruating for the first time, in particular, is a very dramatic experience. The changes in boys are slower, later and less extreme. Facial hair does not become heavy for several years. Their voices break, which is probably the most noticeable change and often embarrasses them, particularly when expected to sing in a youth fellowship. The most alarming development is probably the wet dream or nocturnal emission. But that does not leave the telltale stains that a girl's menstrual flow does. So a boy's development into manhood is less clear cut both to himself and to others.

The age at which puberty begins varies enormously among perfectly normal children of both sexes. In boys, it may begin as early as ten or as late as sixteen. So one boy may have almost completed his physical development before another has even begun.

Many of today's young people are experiencing puberty at an age that may take adults by surprise. This trend contributes to the stresses and strains of the adolescent period, when young people find things happening to their bodies which often no one has prepared them for.

The law

There is also confusion at the other end of this period. Our society has no universally-accepted 'rite of passage' from childhood into the adult world. We do not send our young males out into the jungle for four days alone and allow them to return as adults if they survive (although National Service did fulfil this role to some extent). Instead the law admits young people to a range of activities at a bewildering variety of ages.

There are at least forty-six different things permitted by law at various points between the ages of ten and twenty-one. At ten a child can be arrested by the police and detained for enquiries. At thirteen a child can be employed with limited hours and conditions. At fourteen a young person can be required to have his or her fingerprints taken without parental consent. At fifteen a young person can open a Giro account. At sixteen a young person can enter a mental hospital as a voluntary patient. At seventeen a young person may engage in street trading, or drive a car. At eighteen a young person may be tattooed and has the right to vote. So it goes on, until at twenty-one a person may adopt a child, or stand as a candidate in an election.

Legally we spread the process of entering adulthood over more than a decade. So a young person's status is often ambiguous. He or she may be old enough to get married, but not to watch certain films.

Confusion

As society provides no clear guidelines on the matter, a number of unofficial milestones emerge as significant for the young person: smoking, drinking, 'soft' drug taking, kissing, having a regular boyfriend or girlfriend, buying a bra, growing pubic hair, having to shave, the first period, having an encounter with the police, holidaying apart from parents, holidaying with the boyfriend or girlfriend, and many more. *But the most significant single sign of entering the adult world is seen by the adolescents themselves as obtaining regular employment.*[3]

With youth unemployment figures that climb every time they are published, we now have not only the longest period of adolescence in human history, but also the most confusing. Young people enter puberty earlier and earlier. But unemployment may bar them from their one certain way out of adolescence into adulthood. They enter a period from which they may never emerge—or from which society may never acknowledge that they have emerged. And there lies a problem.

Adulthood is the aspirational goal of all young people, but they do not know exactly 'how' they will become adults.[4] Since society will not tell them clearly when and how they have become adult, young people have to make their own way into the adult world and to announce their own arrival. Not surprisingly they often try to do so prematurely. A communication problem arises.[5]

The young person has put together a set of symbols of adulthood. These will be determined by his culture, but they may well include smoking, drinking, swearing, driving, sexual intercourse, independence from parents. He adopts these symbols and expects the adult world to accept him into its society.

But all too often these superficial, external symbols of adulthood are accompanied by more significant symbols of immaturity. It might be the social uncertainty signalled by loud talk or gang behaviour (the adolescent still loses himself in the gang and refuses to become an individual). So society ignores the symbols and responds to the behavioural reality. The young person is not treated as grown up.

Frustration ensues. He has tried to communicate his message to society. He has said, 'I am grown up,' by encoding the message in symbols and transmitting them: the all-too-obvious cigarette, exaggerated drunkenness (often put on merely for the sake of the signal), the forcefully driven motorbike or car. As far as he can tell, these are the symbols of adulthood. Why doesn't society get the message?

The answer must be that he was not loud enough. So he turns up the volume: he drives faster, smokes more cigarettes; she uses brighter lipstick and more eyeshadow; they are even later getting home at night, talk more loudly about the party last night and how many got drunk, and are more blatant about sex.

The behaviour springs partly out of this confusion over social status. Interestingly, despite a heavy anti-smoking advertising campaign, the number of eighteen to twenty-four-year-olds smoking cigarettes rose by 7% between 1981 and 1984 (according to a market research survey conducted by National Opinion Polls). As a symbol of adulthood, smoking remains a valuable 'signal' for the confused young person trying to tell society something. But the effect of the advertising has been that each young smoker is generally smoking fewer cigarettes. They accept the link between smoking and serious disease and do not 'need' to smoke; but they do need the signal.

Thus, while our culture provides everyone with the luxury of a period of adjustment, during which we can each come to terms with physical maturity and grown-up responsibility, we are all keen to know when the period is over. When society will not give a clear answer to young people, they are desperate to find out for themselves what point they have reached.

Psychological and sociological development

But it is not just over the age limit of adolescence that there is confusion today. There are also conflicting psychological accounts of this period of development.

Sigmund Freud's daughter Anna expressed one approach: 'Adolescence is by its nature an interruption of peaceful growth' (*Psychoanalytic Study of the Child* 1952). She highlighted the paradoxes of this stage in development.[6]

More recently this view of adolescence has been questioned: 'Normal adolescence is not characterised by storm and stress and disturbance'; 'Most young people go through their teenage years without significant behavioural or emotional problems' (Michael Rutter, *Changing Youth in a Changing Society* 1979).[7] This forms a sharp contrast to the widely-accepted idea of the generation gap and of child-parent conflict as 'normal' features of adolescence.

John Nicholson has written:

Interestingly, there is closer agreement on the really important issues between today's teenagers and their parents than between the parents and *their* parents (i.e. the present generation of grandparents), which suggests that if anything the generation gap is closing. The great majority of adolescents say that they are satisfied and happy at home (three quarters of them even express general approval of their parents' approach to discipline), and most of them name their parents when asked whom they admire most in the world. Moreover, two of the fears most frequently expressed by adolescents are of their parents dying and of moving away from home.

This is not to deny that adolescents are influenced by the approval of their friends, but most researchers agree that the influence of peers is stronger than that of parents only when it comes to such matters as clothes, records and what is the most profitable way to spend a Saturday evening (*Seven Ages* p.79).[8]

In research into adolescent values (*Disclosures to a Stranger,* Routledge & Kegan Paul 1980), Tom Kitwood highlighted a number of significant omissions from the material gathered by the research. Certain themes were emphasized more than had been anticipated by the researchers, such as 'domesticity, relationships, reputations, personal achievement and affiliation with the adult world'. But more striking were the omissions.

The most obvious was discussion of the content either of television programmes or of pop music in shaping young people's values. Of television Kitwood wrote:

> There was virtually no indication . . . of boys and girls attributing learning, growth of understanding, interest, concern or satisfaction to its influence. The situation is rather similar with pop music . . . Thus both television and pop music generally seem to form part of the 'background noise' against which more dramatic episodes were enacted (p.113).

Considering the enormous sale of records and cassettes to the teenage market and the well-documented evidence on television-watching by teenagers, it is interesting that they themselves do not see their values as being shaped by television or pop music. It may be that these media are all the more influential on young people because they do not perceive the influence and therefore do not evaluate it.

Kitwood's second significant absence was:

> A general lack of concern about or involvement in ideas as such, even among those who are academically very successful . . . Adolescence is sometimes portrayed, particularly by writers in the psychoanalytic tradition, as a period when some persons will show an intense interest in the affairs of the intellect, an eager searching for a philosophy by which to live, and for ideals in the light of which to strive for a better world. That kind of image is not confirmed by this research (p.114).

> A third absence is frequent and direct reference to sexuality as a source of significance. One of the most commonly held stereotypes of adolescence is that this is a period of intense preoccupation with the physical aspects of sex (p.115).

Kitwood's findings suggested that we may well tend to exaggerate this.

> Fourth, there is little evidence in this research that would support the idea that a 'search for identity' is a major feature of adolescence, at least up to the ages of about eighteen (p.117).

No doubt his findings are open to dispute, but they serve to warn us against the dangers of generalization and stereotyping. He continues:

> any stereotype of contemporary adolescents as being typically in revolt against their parents is incorrect; and there is at least an indication that middle-class girls are the group for whom conflict with parents is most frequent . . . The picture conveyed . . . that adolescent groups exhibit some kind of organic unity, aligned against, or at least indifferent to, the adult world is not supported by this enquiry.[9]

Such findings challenge preconceptions about youth and provide further healthy warning of the dangers of generalization.

Growing up in late twentieth-century society is not a tidy process. There are no neat and comprehensive accounts of it. It is no surprise that the experts disagree. Commonsense observations and the findings of careful research do not always match. Young people are primarily individuals, not members of a tribe. They are part of the same complicated, stress-filled world as the rest of us.

The underside

The experience of growing up today varies sharply according to the social and economic background of the individual. Teenagers in Bromley and teenagers in Brixton (or those in Bebington and Birkenhead) may be only a few miles apart geographically, but they will have very different experiences of the route into adulthood. There may be a wider diversity of experience between one teenager and another than between one generation and another.

Between 1955 and 1975 there was the greatest period of economic growth in the history of civilization. Most of the benefits of that growth were enjoyed by the Western World, but they were not used to narrow the differential between those at the top of the pile and those at the bottom. Despite the affluence enjoyed by the upper and middle classes of British society, there remained a sector of society which never received its invitation to the party.

The comfortable prosperity of suburbia blinded most of the nation to what was happening in the inner-cities. The Department of the Environment uses eight factors to calculate the degree of deprivation of Urban Priority Areas: unemployment, overcrowded households, single-parent households, households lacking exclusive use of basic amenities, pensioners living alone, population change, high mortality rate and households whose head was born in Pakistan or the New Commonwealth. The cumulative effect of such multiple deprivation was seen in the inner-city riots of the summer of

1981 and the quieter echoes of 1985 (although significantly more violent—the first use of a gun in a riot in mainland Great Britain was in Tottenham in September 1985).

For the adolescent, one of these factors outweighs all others; unemployment.[10] For the young person growing up with a sense of powerlessness and disadvantage and inferiority, the experience of unemployment comes as one further catastrophic blow to self-esteem. The sense of being on the underside, statusless and exploited in a society where others enjoy greater and greater affluence, is bitter. As society's values become more and more materialistic, those who are cooped up in inner-city 'reservations', and cut off from enjoying the material prosperity that they see paraded all around them by media advertising, may well resort to crime and violence to obtain the goals that all society worships. No other legitimate way of reaching these goals is open to them.

The Police Commissioner present at the Tottenham riot in September 1985 said he saw three significant things that night. First, there was excitement in an area where most young people do not even smile and have few occasions to get excited. Then there was material gain from looting—in some cases substantial gain, and of high-priced and heavily-advertised goods like videos and computers. Third, there was the opportunity for power—to express physical aggression against the rest of society by fighting the police.

This pressure certainly appears to affect young men in the inner-city more than young women, although an increasing number of young women are becoming criminal. Youth workers are also noticing a trend among young, unmarried women to get pregnant—so that they can answer that threatening question, 'What do you do?' by saying, 'I'm a mum; I look after my child,' and to gain independence by obtaining a council flat.

A new fact of life

Youth unemployment on its present massive scale is something that society has not yet adjusted to.[11] But it would appear to be here to stay. It has been calculated that:

> the solution of Britain's unemployment demands an increase in the gross National Product greater than any Western nation has achieved since the war, simply to restore employment levels to those of the sixties. Britain is hardly likely to achieve it (Tom Sine, *The Mustard Seed Conspiracy,* Marc Europe 1981, p.55).

Unemployment is a new fact of life for the urban young.[12] No one yet knows the full consequences of this alarming truth. 'The problem of how to structure social life and maintain self-esteem when unemployed is still largely to be resolved' (Kitwood).[13]

But there are signs that young people are tackling the task of living with unemployment with some resilience:

> Adjustment is best in areas where unemployment has become a normal experience, where it binds friends together. Such young people move in and out of Government schemes and unskilled low wage jobs, in a series of experiences which (has been termed) 'sub-employment' . . .
>
> Psychological well-being slumps when jobs are lost, and continues to deteriorate as jobless spells lengthen. The majority regard joblessness as a problem. They dislike the boredom that it creates.
>
> However . . . they are not so demoralised that any low paid job or underpaid Government scheme is acceptable. Nor are they scarred for life . . . instead the young are coping with unemployment as an unpleasant fact of life (*Youthaid* Bulletin No.6).[14]

'Sub-employment' is how young people perceive government schemes intended to alleviate the pressure of school leavers on the dole queues. As soon as it has any element of coercion, the Youth Training Scheme is seen as a virtual raising of the school leaving age, rather than as an acceptable doorway into the adult world. The young cannot be fooled into ascribing to it a status which it clearly does not have in the eyes of the rest of society.

Unemployment and the new phenomenon of 'sub-employment' are not significant just for the older teenager. Those affected by them are now well up into their twenties. 'The acute anxieties of adolescence often give way, not to full "citizenship" but to a chronic condition of helplessness and hopelessness in young adulthood: a crisis both reflecting and creating the symbolic prolonging of youth' (Howard Williamson, *Youth in Society* January 1985). We do not yet know what harvest society will eventually reap from this sowing of youth unemployment. It is an obstacle in the path of many young people's psychological development. We have not yet seen the full extent of the consequences.

A grim backcloth

It is against this grim backcloth that the more sensational problems of disadvantaged young people must be viewed. Drug abuse, football hooliganism, glue-sniffing, mugging, vandalism and riots are more newsworthy, but they are probably less significant than what is happening economically to the poorer echelons of society as Britain moves away from full employment, possibly for ever. It is impossible to review the situation of young people in British society at the end of the twentieth century without concluding that youth unemployment is the dominant feature of this period of development.

Unemployment casts fresh light on other 'youth statistics'. In 1982, for example, over 350,000 cars were stolen, almost always by males, and three-quarters of those convicted were under twenty-one years old. Handling a car is a symbol of adult status, but no one can afford to run a car on the dole. So taking and driving away someone else's car can be yet another way an unemployed young person tries to tell his world that he is grown up, when that world will not let him join adult society by the orthodox route of paid employment. (In 1985 there was an epidemic of 'joy-riding' among teenagers in Dublin, where employment prospects are particularly bleak.)

As youth unemployment rises, so there will be more and

more young people shut out of society. The increase will be uneven; young blacks are twice as likely to be unemployed as young whites. Girls get a rougher deal than boys. There is a disproportionate concentration in the inner-cities. There it may cause explosions of riot, arson and looting. It may fuel political extremism, as the National Front and the hard left feed on the alienated. Or it may simply remove any youthful zest for life, as young men stay in bed until noon or later, 'doss around' in the shopping mall, watch videos late into the night, look forward to drawing the dole as the high point of their week, and conclude that they are the unwanted margins of society.

The marginalized young people of the urban areas are not the only young people suffering from injustice in Britain. Young people in rural areas experience quite different forms of deprivation, and they also have urgent needs. There is often a lack of local provision for them and a lack of transport to reach better-equipped areas. Their isolation and wide diffusion mean their protests are not heard.[15]

The need for perspective

The situation is complex. When we talk of the poor and dis-advantaged of the inner-cities and council estates, we are speaking in comparative terms. No one in Britain today is poor on a world-wide scale of riches and poverty. The Third World (or Two-Thirds World) experiences poverty of a sort that puts the most severely socially and economically de-pressed communities in Britain into a luxurious perspective. It is important to retain that perspective.

There is, however, a poverty of powerlessness. When most people grow richer in a culture besotted with materialism, those left behind will feel socially and economically op-pressed. When they find that the way up and out of their situation has been barred to them by factors that are out of their control and beyond their understanding, then there is real injustice. When young men take to the streets in Toxteth and Brixton, and Handsworth and Tottenham, every Christian should have some sense of the corporate sin that has contributed to the cause of those riots.

But historically the Christian faith has often appeared ineffective in penetrating the lower classes of Western industrial nations.[16] Those who sense that society has given them a raw deal also feel alienated from the traditional forms of Christianity. The church has a middle-class image and is accused of having a middle-class bias.

The Archbishop of Canterbury's Commission on Urban Priority Areas published its report in December 1985, and noted:

> there are sizeable groups of young people who are trapped in UPAs, who only gain attention when they become a threat, who are denied equality of opportunity and life chances, and with whom the churches have little or no contact. It is difficult to exaggerate how alienated these young people are: from adult ideas of how young people should behave; from their peers of different social classes; from agencies they think of as acting on adults' behalf and not usually in the interests of young people, e.g. from the police; from school; and from the Church (*Faith In The City,* Church House Publishing 1985, p.315).

Here too there is complexity. It is true that the Christian church has rarely been true to its Master in showing 'a preferential option for the poor' (1980 Puebla Conference of Latin American Bishops). No longer can its members say, along with the earliest disciples, 'Silver and gold have I none'— which may explain why they cannot echo the rest of that famous saying—'but I give you what I have; in the name of Jesus Christ of Nazareth rise up and walk!'

There is, therefore, a welcome call today for the church to be much more faithful in reflecting God's passionate concern for the needy and the deprived. That concern will express itself wherever it encounters oppression. It will not stop to consider whether the oppression can really be considered serious on a world-wide perspective. As the government tries to practise positive discrimination in support of disadvantaged areas, so should the church (and often it does not).

The situation in Britain today, however, is that the middle classes owe their existence and their ethos to two main factors: the Industrial Revolution and Christianity. A nation cannot be exposed to the Bible and the public practice of Christianity for centuries without an enormous unseen influence on its manners, customs, attitudes, standards, laws and morals. This is not to say that British society today is especially righteous. Perhaps its most marked features are actually its gross materialism and its increasing secularization. But there has nevertheless been an historical process in which the nation's development has been continuously exposed to the ideas of Jesus Christ.

So the unconscious presuppositions of British society today have been affected by Christianity. Concern for the environment, for free speech, for a neighbour's rights to peace and privacy, for animal welfare, for the disabled, for children, for democracy, for freedom, for honesty and integrity in public life, for justice for minority groups—these and many more, to a greater or lesser extent, owe their origins to the teaching of Christ. They are not apparent in societies conditioned by religions other than Christianity. They are a part of the middle-class ethos of British society. This must not be overstated, but it needs to be said to provide a necessary perspective on the middle-class image of Christianity.

It is not simply the blind economic forces of Marxist philosophy that have shaped society. There are also ideas. In the long run, ideas have a greater influence on people's lives, because we are free agents made in God's image, and not the products of a blind and meaningless evolutionary process. So, when considering the impact of Christianity upon the disadvantaged young people of the inner-city, the complex historical situation in which we live must not be forgotten. Christian ideas may raise a young convert up the social scale. Conversion may actually improve his or her job prospects.

It has been said that the Holy Spirit converts someone and then the church makes them middle-class. There may be some truth in this, but things are more complicated than that. Certain middle-class values are Christian values and the new convert will acquire them. He or she will also lose some working-class values that are not Christian.

But it is vital that the new convert should not acquire a whole set of further middle-class values that have nothing to do with Christ, or lose working-class values (like the community solidarity of a neighbourhood, the closeness of the family, and the importance of the immediate) which are more Christ-like than the middle-class values that replace them (like material self-improvement). Conversion will inevitably distance every Christian from his or her social class. It is not just the influence of a worldly, bourgeois church.

Only a part

For the many young people who experience the underside of life in our society, adolescence can exaggerate their sense of being statusless, powerless and deprived. It may alienate them from Christianity, but there is a danger that we fail to view these things in a balanced perspective.

The disadvantaged young people of our society are especially close to the heart of Jesus Christ and for that reason the church must have a special concern for them, otherwise it will not be true to a God who delights to lift up the humble and put down the mighty, who 'raises the poor from the dust and lifts the needy from the ash heap' (1 Sam 2:8; Ps 113:7). But they are not normative when considering adolescence today. They are only a part of the picture. They must not so dominate our thinking that they lead it into caricature and exaggeration as we seek an overview of young people today.

For example, although youth unemployment is a new and alarming development, the young may actually be the best equipped to cope with the psychological consequences of unemployment. They are more resilient in creating social and psychological mechanisms to cope with the assault on their self-esteem. Appalling as the prospect of youth unemployment is, it is probably better than a huge increase in middle-age unemployment. It would be no solution to cure youth unemployment by creating unemployment elsewhere in society. The challenge before the British government at the end of the twentieth century is to alter the nation's attitude to work and unemployment so as to create a society in which every member can feel valued for what he or she can contribute to the common good.

So it is important to view adolescence in the context of our whole society and culture. We have seen that there are grounds for doubting the popular picture of it as a period of turmoil and stress, characterized by a rejection of adult values and a commitment to the peer group at the expense of good relationships with parents. Such generalizations are dangerous because they tend to stereotype the individual young person and they do not allow for the variety of adolescent experience. We have also seen that different young people are growing up into very different environments. While we must never forget the disadvantaged, any analysis of adolescence in our society must also take into account the large numbers of young people growing up today with 'advantages' never known to their predecessors.

Blood Brothers to King Kong or Members of the Human Race?

Adolescence in late twentieth-century Western society (ii)

Their world is our world

Young people live in their world, but they also live in our world. Youth culture is our culture. We will not understand it until we begin to understand ourselves. We cannot single out extreme manifestations of youth culture and use them to build up a picture of the odd and alien nature of the young, unless we are also prepared to look at our own adult world and see where these eccentricities came from. The excesses of adolescence are only a distorted reflection of our own value system.

This point was well made by Robert Elms:

Before the teen explosion of the Fifties and Sixties, young people were simply old people in smaller sizes. Now it is precisely the other way round, nobody is a teenager any more because everybody is . . .

What was once called youth culture, and before that pop culture, is now simply popular culture, everybody's doing it . . .

Live Aid was hardly the celebration of the power of youth that it has been painted, half of the performers were old enough to be the parents of the other half ('Time to wake up from the teen dream', *Sunday Times* 12 January 1986).

So drug abuse by young people needs to be seen in the context of a drug-taking society. In Britain about 5,000 drugs, comprising some 1,500 medical substances, can be prescribed. About 400 of these act on the brain and nervous system. We are all accustomed to the use of drugs in our everyday life and we think nothing of resorting to them frequently to help us through the aches and pains that beset us. The busy housewife who takes Veganin to stave off a migraine, or the nervous executive who is on Valium to keep him from depression, are only different in degree from the disillusioned sixteen-year-old with no prospects for employment who sniffs glue to help him through the day.

Drug abuse has been described by the Home Office as 'the most serious peacetime threat to the national well-being'. In 1984 there were 5,370 new registered addicts, of which 90% were heroin users. Drug addiction is a terrible thing, particularly among the young, but heroin is actually less addictive than nicotine, and heroin addicts can give up more easily than alcoholics. One withdrawal symptom with which most people are acquainted is the common hangover. We must never lose sight of ourselves as drug-takers when we start to analyse drug abuse among the young. We only understand what is happening to the young when we understand what is happening to their parents.

We live in a peculiar age here in the Western World, having largely removed pain, disease and death from our everyday experience.

A British surgeon visiting Africa found himself faced with a young girl who needed her appendix removed urgently. She was lying naked on a table under a sixty watt light bulb, waiting for him to operate with only local anaesthetic. Expecting the patient to be nervous and distressed, the surgeon took her pulse. To his surprise, it was normal.

Then he realized that her everyday expectation of living was that it would include pain. The prospect of pain did not distress her as it would a Westerner. The pain of the operation would in time ease the pain of the appendicitis. Both were accepted as 'normal' experiences.

It is the Western World that is 'abnormal' in this respect. We are amazed to encounter societies that still treat pain and death in as matter-of-fact a way as our ancestors did. It is we who are peculiar. There are a number of other features of our contemporary culture which have special implications for young people growing into adulthood. These are primarily aspects of adult society, but they demand comment because of the influence they have on youth culture. Often that influence results in an exaggeration or a distortion of the original feature.

The spoilt children of the planet

One example would be that green hair-dye, Mohican hair-styles and other excesses of youth fashion only make sense against the background of the desperate materialistic con-sumerism of our society.

We are the spoilt children of our planet, racing through its resources at a terrifying speed. Back in 1966 Malcolm Muggeridge caricatured the British post-war dream.

> Wealth increasing forever more, and its beneficiaries, rich in hire-purchase, stupified with the telly and with sex, comprehensively educated, told by Professor Hoyle how the world began and by Bertrand Russell where it will end; venturing forth on the broad highways, three lanes a side . . . blood spattering the tarmac as an extra thrill; heaven lying about them in the supermarket, the rainbow ending in the nearest bingo hall, leisure burgeoning out in multitudinous shining aerials rising like dreaming spires into the sky (article in *The Observer* 26 June 1966).

This dream is devoted to an emphatic belief that a man's life *does* consist in the abundance of his possessions, that happiness is linked to how much we accumulate. The 'good life' is defined in terms of consumerism, materialism, the pursuit of power, and self-realization. The dream has effectively corrupted our thinking so that our concern for the victims of Third World disasters is not applied practically to the lifestyles we ourselves pursue.

> Those who anguish over a starving mankind on the easy assumpt-ion that there just is not enough land and resources to feed the hungry, might do well to pay a special kind of visit to their local supermarket. Not to shop, but to observe and to meditate on what they see before them and had always taken for granted. How much of the world's land and labour was wasted producing the tobacco, the coffee, the tea, the refined cane sugars, the pol-ished rice, the ice-cream, the candies, the cookies, the soft drinks, the thousand and one non-nutritional luxuries one finds there? The grain that became liquor, the fruit and vegetables that lost all their food value going into cans and jars full of syrup and condi-ments, the potatoes and corn that became various kinds of chips, crackles, crunchies, and yum-yums, the cereals that became breakfast novelties less nourishing (as a matter of scientific fact) than the boxes they are packed in, the wheat that became white bread and pastry flours . . . how many forests perished to package these non-foods? How many resources went into transporting and processing them? (And the less nutrition, the more processing). How much skilled energy went into advertising and merchandis-ing them? There they stand in our markets, row upon row, aisle upon aisle of nutritional zero, gaily boxed and packed, and cost-ing those fancy prices we then gripe about as the high cost of living (Theodore Roszak).[17]

Advertisers in the West face a difficult task. They have to persuade people, who already have everything they need, that they want what they do not need. Unless they achieve this, the economy would collapse. So the advertising industry works to reverse society's values. Material things are sold to people who have no material needs on the grounds that they will meet spiritual needs. A certain product will bring love, harmony and friendship into the lives of those who possess it.

Certain clothes will make their wearer likeable, or adult. A certain soft drink will make the whole world sing in perfect harmony. Spiritual values are attached to material products. On the other hand, what used to be considered the seven deadly sins have all (with the exception of sloth) been turned into positive virtues: greed, avarice, envy, gluttony, luxury and pride are the driving forces of our economy.

Young people are both seduced and repelled by this materialism. It is flattering to be wooed by the advertisers for the uncommitted spending money in their pockets. So the young collude with the commercial exploitation of themselves by the fashion, music and entertainment industries. They buy the designer jeans that are so heavily promoted. But they also sense the sham.

They know that 'a leisure life centred on TV, drink, drugs and fantasy sex is no basis at all for the development of free people' (Prof. David Marsland in *Youth in Society* March 1985). They detect the hollow dream of the hedonistic Playboy philosophy, where life is a playground and people are playmates. They want to grow out of 'Kiddy City' and are not fooled when adult life is portrayed with the topsy-turvy values of the advertising industry.

They may not express their idealism in the protest songs of earlier generations. Today youthful protest at the materialistic values of the older generation takes different forms from the powerful lyrics of the early 1960s, from writers like Bob Dylan, who sang out in memorable fashion that 'the times they are a-changin''.

But that idealism is still present, and still at war with the materialism of the 'overdeveloped' Western World. The young are torn by the same value conflict that afflicts adult society, but their experience of it is more immediate and often more extreme.

The black youths, who loot leather jackets from Burtons in Brixton during a riot, and their teenage contemporaries in Bromley, who work desperately to achieve the academic grades necessary to obtain good jobs and to satisfy their parents' ambitions, are both driven by the same acquisitive materialism. The same value system has pervaded urban and suburban society: a man's life consists in the abundance of his possessions.

However, the zeal with which young people will espouse a cause—whether it is animal rights, CND, vegetarianism, solidarity with Polish Trades Unions, or Live Aid—reveals that this pervasive materialistic philosophy has not crushed the idealism out of them. Youth is not only concerned with pleasure—it is also an age of idealism.

The 'nuclear' family

Teenage cults and fashions, however bizarre they may appear, are only a symptom of a society in which people live as though material things are of supreme importance. This religion of personal well-being has had other, far-reaching effects.

Sociologists suggest that one reason for the appearance of the nuclear family (Mum and Dad plus a couple of kids, separated from other relatives) is that children are 'economically disfunctional'. In other words, it is no longer financially beneficial to have more children. In fact it is very expensive to have them. They put our standard of living in jeopardy. So we have started having fewer children. The nuclear family has emerged, as a result of the Western World's preoccupation with its own lifestyle.

Clearly other factors have contributed over many decades to the disappearance of the extended family, but the result is that few people in British society now live close to large numbers of their blood-relatives. A price has had to be paid for this sociological change.

Dr Benjamin Spock's book, *Babycare,* came out in Britain in paperback in 1945. It sold more copies than any previous book in the history of the world, other than the Bible. The reason is clear. In every other age and in most other cultures the young mother has had an abundance of older female relatives ready and eager to participate in the process of child-birth and baby care, but suddenly in post-war Western society young women found themselves facing one of the most daunting prospects of human experience without the advice and help of those who had been through it before. So they bought Dr Spock.

That is one example of the stresses induced by the demise of the extended family. Small families are much more intense in the emotional pressures that are exerted on the individual members. They do not have the resources that are available in a larger family unit to cope with stress, strain, trauma and tension. Conflict between members of the nuclear family is more psychologically damaging, because it cannot be diffused among a wider group who have a permanent and unbreakable commitment to one another.

The family has a complicated role in the development of the teenager. It provides a haven in a heartless world, but it also provides a dumping ground where emotion can be poured out on the other members, without the possibility of permanent rejection. Teenagers 'need' their families even when they do not want them, and for many, family life is both an agonizing and a joyful experience at the same time.

Of course, many teenagers do not have a family life to speak of. Not only are families shrinking in size, but they are also fragmenting. Only one third of British households contain families with children, but one in every eight of these will be single-parent households. Most teenagers today will be members of small families, and many will be members of only a part of a small family.

We do not have the scope here to consider in detail the link between materialism and divorce, but as Western culture has become more preoccupied with materialistic goals, so the rate of marital breakdown has rocketed up. The divorce rate in England and Wales has risen by 600% in the last twenty years.

This has deeply affected the young. The link between juvenile crime and the absence of a father at home is strong.[18]

Some research suggests that even an unjust and violent father, who comes home drunk and who frightens the whole family, provides a more healthy environment for the psychological development of the adolescent male than the absence of any male authority figure in the family. The young male has a need to discover boundaries, to encounter limits which he cannot cross. When these limits are missing, his development into a responsible adult is seriously jeopardized.

The effects of the small or incomplete family on young people have not yet been fully documented. They will possibly prove to be more extensive than we yet imagine. It is something new in the history of Western man.

The video revolution

Another feature of our adult world that has a particular impact on the young is the revolution in the media. Once again we do not yet know what is happening to the minds of young people as a result of the constant input of television and video. We *do* know how much they are watching: it is estimated at up to twenty-seven hours a week.

A more conservative estimate came in a letter to a national newspaper from a headmaster in June 1985:

> If a child between the ages of six and sixteen watches television two hours a day for the duration of this intellectually formative period, he invests seven thousand three hundred hours of his time in the medium. This represents something like fifteen percent of his waking life spent in front of the TV set (*The Times* 27 June 1985).

The letter went on to make the point that it is not the content of the programmes watched that may be educationally damaging, but the medium itself.

However, the report of the Parliamentary Group Video Inquiry (*Video Violence and Children* 1985)[19] provided evidence for a direct link between the watching of video nasties and violent behaviour and distorted views of sex among young people.

> Some children and young people are addicted to violence in much the same way as they are becoming hooked on drugs, only this is even worse. There is strong evidence that children copy what they see on the screen (Dr Clifford Hill, Consultant Sociologist to the Home Office and director of the inquiry).

Another member of the inquiry said,

> One little girl came to me and said she now knew all about sex because of a video she had seen. She said it was about a big man holding down a lady and the lady had screamed and screamed and screamed (*The Times* 17 October 1985).

The inquiry also published a survey in which 45% of the young people over seven years old questioned had seen at least one video nasty. The NSPCC estimate that over 70% of fifteen- and sixteen-year-old boys have seen four or more '18' rated video films.[20]

The availability of this material is a key point. Young people have easy access to it. But once again it is important not to focus on the alarming and sensational, and ignore what is far more fundamental: we are a TV-watching society. Young people are only copying their parents. It is simply that the young have more leisure time to do it. The television screen is more and more dominant in all our lives.

It is hard to calculate the full extent of its impact on us.[21] We have already considered the rampant materialism of contemporary society. We have to remember that this materialism has a propaganda medium of unknown power at its disposal. As J.K. Galbraith said of modern man and advertising, 'On no other matter religious, political or moral is he so elaborately instructed' *(The New Industrial State).*

The ultimate consequences of this revolution in communication must be enormous. There is an end to innocence when television begins to strip away the possibility of secrecy from childhood. It initiates the young into aspects of life that have been kept from them in previous ages. They used to be thought too tender for certain information (usually about sex and violence), and this would be excluded from children's reading. Now that television rather than reading has become the major medium of communication, everything that adults know via television, children also know via the same medium.

The advent of literacy in the Western World helped to undermine respect for the old, because in a non-literate society the old are the repositories of all knowledge. Now, in a similar way the advent of television has begun to remove the possibility of an age of innocence. It threatens to abolish childhood. (It may even have begun to undermine literacy, as communication becomes more visual and immediate and there is a lower premium on the ability to read and to write.)

Fantasy has always been more attractive to the young than reality, but it is now becoming more 'real'. The fast-changing images of the television screen present the young with a more 'interesting' experience than their real lives. The technical sophistication of television advertising has already made the commercials more interesting than the programmes. The primary school teacher is competing with *Sesame Street* for the attention of her pupils. She can only draw the letter 'P' on the blackboard. Her pupils are expecting it to dance and sing, and become the hero in a cartoon story.

When American teenage boys were asked to choose between the possibility of never watching television for the rest of their lives, and of never speaking to their fathers again, the majority chose never to speak to their fathers. This is hardly surprising when they are watching television for several hours a day, and only speaking to their fathers on average for a matter of a few minutes.

The alarming thought is that we do not know the end of this process. We know how much television is being watched, and we know what sort of television is being watched. Along with the popularity of video nasties and '18' rated films (among those who get access to them), a survey of TV watching by fourteen- to sixteen-year-olds in 1984 concluded:

Soap operas lead the way with thirty four percent; drama and adventure series (not including any plays) follow with thirty one percent (police and crime series accounting for two thirds of the total). Then there's a big drop to twelve percent (music, mainly Top Of The Pops), eight percent (comedy), four percent (children's programmes), and three percent (sport, mainly voted by boys). The remaining eight percent is a mixed bag of chat shows, games show and the like, but also includes the only informative and educational elements mentioned (John Allan in *The Harvester* 1985).

John Allan summed up that survey: 'Escape and unreality are the key notes of teenage TV watching at the moment.' A survey of adult TV watching might draw the same conclusion.

It is not the sensational consequences of teenagers watching *Return of the Living Dead* or *Zombie Flesh-Eaters* that we should find most worrying. It is the 'normal' effect of 'normal' television watching by 'normal' people, young and old. It certainly does affect us. There would not be so much advertising money poured into television if it did not have the power to change our behaviour. The young are likely to be particularly susceptible. No one controls and no one can predict its influence. One headmaster spoke of children forming ranks in the playground and charging each other in a re-enactment of the miners' strike.

No doubt we can exaggerate the influence of television on young people. I have already mentioned research into adolescent values which found they attributed very little to the influence of television. There is also the temptation to sensationalize the statistics about video nasties and pornography. Indeed the young frequently suffer from distortion and exaggeration in the media's reporting of their activities. (Bradford University's Social Work Research Unit conducted an analysis of media reporting on young people in 1979. They found that the most newsworthy aspect of young people was their involvement in crime.)

Television is a new medium of communication and we do

not entirely perceive its influence upon us. That influence is not confined to the young. It is not that TV is good for adults but dangerous for children. It is probably dangerous for all of us in some respect, and beneficial in others. Once again we need to look critically at ourselves before we pass superficial judgement on the young.

The great big melting pot

The impact of television should have made youth culture more homogenous, as young people all over the country follow the same soap operas, are bombarded by the same advertisements and listen to the same music. Popular music certainly has been a unifying force in teenage culture.[22] But the declining popularity of programmes like *Top Of The Pops* and *The Tube* suggests that music is losing this power. No longer do one or two bands (or even musical styles) have universal popularity. The range of musical tastes among young people grows wider every year.

In fact young people are growing up in a more culturally mixed society than ever. They are more aware of this than their parents. For example, they will be taught religion at school as a very different subject from the one their fathers and mothers were taught. If some of the syllabus sinks in, they may well have read parts of the Qu'ran, be familiar with the five pillars of Islam, and know more of the life of the prophet Mohammad than they know of the life of Jesus Christ.

It is not only at school that they will encounter ideas from other world religions. Cult members in the high street and even the lyrics of some songs may confront them with the foundational ideas of Hinduism and Buddhism.

These challenge Western thinking at its core. A fundamental principle of Western thinking is analysis and classification through the use of reason. This depends on the separation of myself (as the knower) from the thing I am investigating (the known). For Eastern thought that distinction is *Maya* (illusion). The basic religious quest is to find release from this diversity and separation by experiencing the essential oneness of the universe with myself. For young people sickened by the shallow materialistic obsessions of Western society the idea of penetrating the sham of appearances to find the spiritual reality beneath has great appeal.

School children may be learning a better understanding of, and a greater respect for, one of the other world religions than for Christianity. The young are less likely than the old to show an attitude of dismissive ignorance to other faiths. They are not being taught at school to despise other religions. The Christian faith is only one among a number competing for their allegiance in the ideological market place. (So it will not commend itself by scorning competing world views. It must take them seriously and answer them honestly, if it is to win the respect of the young in order to gain a fair hearing for itself.)

There are about half a million Hindus, a million Muslims and something like two hundred thousand Sikhs in Britain today. There are roughly twice as many Muslims in Britain as there are Christians in Pakistan. Leicester is reputedly the largest Hindu city outside India. We are sensitive to the need for tolerance and acceptance if our society is to hold together, but even this sensitivity can cause some complex tensions.

The tolerance that respects Islam and Hinduism often goes with strong feelings about other issues of social justice, like feminism. But a concern for women's rights will soon conflict with a concern to respect an Asian community.

For the Muslim, Hindu, or Sikh woman, the home and family, bringing up the children and initiating them into their religion and culture, are the primary responsibilities. The man's concerns are the wider family relationships and providing for the family's economic and material well-being. In some spheres of life the two sexes will actually be physically segregated—at social functions, in the mosque (if they are Muslim), even the household may be divided into separate male and female domains if 'purdah' is observed.

The arranged marriage plays an important part in such a system. The normal assumption among most young people today would be that an arranged marriage must be a recipe for disaster, but the track record of arranged marriages is no worse than that of 'romantic' marriages.[23]

In 1977 a minister at the Foreign and Commonwealth Office addressing the then Select Committee on Race Relations said, 'We would want to discourage the arranged marriage system . . . we hope that more and more parents will respect the rights of their children.' Such a remark revealed the minister's Western values.

> The very concept of individualism which runs throughout Western culture directly contradicts the fundamental characteristics of the Asian communities, where communal values dominate and the extended family is the basic social unit (Shams-Ud-Deen Hassan in *Youth in Society* June 1985).

Customs which a Western feminist would take to be a denial of basic human freedoms are part of the fabric of societies far more stable than our own.

As a minority in the UK, the Asian communities may appear 'abnormal', but world-wide they are 'normal' and the Western way of doing things is peculiar. Our attitude to love and marriage is comparatively recent in human history (it appeared in Europe in the eleventh century) and is still mainly confined to Western industrialized society. 'Elsewhere and at other times, marriage has been seen as a business contract or an outlet for sexual desire, rather than as a source of emotional gratification' (John Nicholson, *Seven Ages* p. 121).

Finding a mate and choosing a career are two of the developmental tasks that face young people entering adulthood. Both of them are tasks that young people in other ages have not been expected to handle by themselves.

Some immigrant communities serve to highlight this peculiarity of our society, because they too exercise much firmer control over these aspects of a young person's life. It is interesting to note that their culture is much closer to those of the Old and New Testaments than our own. They have valuable lessons to teach us. We must beware of an unconscious superiority if we assume that their culture and traditions will soon be swallowed up by ours. We will all be the poorer if that happens.

The young are growing up in a global village where cultures meet head on. When Mrs Ghandi was assassinated 7,000 miles away in India, Sikhs demonstrated on the streets of Leicester. The rest of the world is now on our doorstep and young people are less likely than their parents to think that a British way of life is normative for the whole globe. They can see that there are other cultures markedly different from ours, cultures that have their own particular strengths and weaknesses. This pluralism encourages the questioning of cultural values, so that the way a Hindu friend at school handles bereavement and grief over the death of a parent may make an Anglo-Saxon teenager question the virtue of the British 'stiff upper lip'.

All the Asian and Afro-Caribbean people living in Britain actually number less than 4% of the population, but there is a greater awareness today of the multi-cultural nature of our society. While this awareness is of benefit to the young, there are also many problems. Most young people would share the nightmare and the dream of the chairman for the Commission for Racial Equality:

> I have been involved in race-relations for 10 years, full-time, or part-time as Minister, Member of Parliament and now Chairman of the Commission. Looking ahead through the 1980s I see a nightmare and dream.
>
> The nightmare is of a nation which has made fair headway in race-relations but now falters from lack of will; a Britain sliding into racial turmoil; our national life poisoned by racial hatred; urban violence escalating; individual despair and alienation deepening; our international reputation tarnished.
>
> The dream is of a Britain having accepted racial justice and

harmony as a major national goal; a confident and cohesive country, made stronger by diverse talents harnessed in a common loyalty; its citizens from the minority communities reaching positions of eminence and power in all walks of life; personal relationships no longer hampered by barriers of race or colour; Britain's traditions of tolerance and fair-play finding fresh expression in this modern multi-racial society (*New Equals* No. 7).

That dream is still a dream and, as the adult generation have struggled with it, so the rising generation will play their part in bringing it to pass, or consigning it to dreamland.

Change is the status quo

A final example of a feature of the modern world that has particular impact on young people is the pace of change. Our society is finding it hard to cope with what Alvin Toffler called 'future shock'. He pointed out that, in the record of human achievement, the halfway point is well within human memory.

He suggested that if we divide the last 50,000 years of man's existence into lifetimes of sixty-two years each, there have been 800 such lifetimes—650 of which were spent in caves. Only during the last seventy lifetimes has it been possible to communicate effectively from one lifetime to another by writing. Only during the last six have masses of people seen the printed word. Only during the last four has it been possible to measure time precisely. Only in the last two have we had electricity. The overwhelming majority of all the goods we use each day have been developed in the last 800th lifetime. Man has achieved almost as much since I was born (1948), as he achieved in all the centuries before my birth!

We have not realized what is happening to us. Change always happens faster than society expects. At the beginning of the 1960s Ladbroke's were asked to accept a bet that a man would stand on the surface of the moon before the end of the decade. No one at the time would have thought the bookmaker over-generous in offering odds of one thousand to one against. But I imagine the punter wished he had staked more than £10 when he collected his winnings, with five months to spare!

The record of human achievement climbs exponentially year by year. Since the Second World War, for the first time in history, parents have been unable to help children with their homework because the children are learning things the parents do not yet (and maybe never will) understand.

For the young people themselves this future shock has meant that the past grows increasingly distant from the present. Just to imagine a world without television is a difficult task. Social changes that would have taken a century now occur in less than a generation. So the past seems progressively more remote and irrelevant.

But at the same time the future too grows more uncertain. Aware of the speed of change, and its unpredictable direction, young people today are growing into a world that is more unknowable than that confronted by any previous generation. They cannot anticipate what sort of society they will face as adults.

So the present assumes a new significance. It alone is relevant, immediate and knowable. Past solutions to life's problems are not necessarily valid in the here-and-now, and no one knows whether today's thinking will be relevant in tomorrow's world. The present has an autonomy quite unknown in more static societies.

So existentialism, with its emphasis on the individual authenticating his or her own existence in the present moment, may seem a more appropriate philosophy of life than Christianity. The old religions do not seem to equip their followers for life in 'technopolis'. Certainly the overwhelming impact of technological change feeds the myth of 'scientism'—the belief that science is providing all the knowledge needed for human life on this planet.

So the young sense that in some way science has disproved, or displaced, religion. It is relevant and practical (where religion prays for rain, science builds a dam), but also awesome and amazing. The popularity of science fiction lies in its ability to celebrate man's ingenuity, while hinting at something infinitely meaningful and fulfilling which remains beyond his grasp. Many young people believe there is more hope for the future in the close encounters that science may provide us with, than in the execution of a Jewish carpenter two thousand years ago.

This future shock may also have contributed to what Harvey Cox has called the new 'gluttony of experience'. Only the present has any certainty, so only in the present can we experience reality. Therefore, we must make the most of present experience. Commitment involves a determined prediction about a future that is quite unknowable here and now. So it is unreasonable to expect a high degree of commitment.

It is not the shadow of the nuclear holocaust that encourages young people to live for the present (because there may be no future). It is the much more certain (and probably subconscious) knowledge that that future will be very different from the present. This is what gives them problems with commitment, and encourages them to maximize the present, 'lived' moment.

Every age in our society is affected by the pace of change. The old find it most painful of all. The young show the greatest flexibility in coping with it. But the young are also the most conditioned by it. They sense that they are accelerating into an uncertain future of bewildering technical achievement, where the possibilities for good and evil will be immense. The one certainty is that we do *not* know what it will be like until we get there.

'I just want to grow up'

By the end of the century the world population will pass six billion, and two billion will be under the age of twenty. In Latin America the number of those under twenty will double in that period and in Africa it will treble. Some countries like Zambia already have 75% of their population under twenty. There will be a significant increase in Europe as well. Most of the factors shaping adolescence, which we have considered in this survey, will become more potent rather than less as the century draws to a close.

But the increase in the number of young people and the powerful forces that will influence them as they pass into adulthood do not change the fact that youth is *a normal and a good period of life*. Young people are members of the same world and the same human race as their parents. They are not scapegoats for the faults and eccentricities of adult society.

They mirror (and exaggerate) some of the aspects of the adult world that the adults themselves would most like to forget about: drug-taking, obsession with material values, violence and crime in response to deprivation and unemployment. But they also exhibit the idealism and enthusiasm that are sometimes in short supply among adults.

We develop a better understanding of the young if we do not view them as a separate and alien tribe. They belong in the context of our whole society, a society more peculiar than we may like to admit, but we cannot pass the buck to the young when it comes to responsibility for those peculiarities.

Just like every other age they have particular developmental tasks which absorb much of their energy. The main goal of young people is to reach adulthood—to be accepted by the adult world as grown up—but they need (and are granted by society) a moratorium in which to develop a sense of confidence and personal worth to face adult life. If that sense is denied them, there will be unfortunate consequences for them and for society.

The fact of young people's youthfulness should be respected. They are in a transitional condition between childhood and adulthood. As they are seeking to establish their own identity, they are strongly influenced by their peer group and by 'significant' adults. They are concerned about their competence in the interpersonal domain.[24] It is very hard for someone under sixteen to hold an individual belief.[25]

Adults sometimes misjudge the young in assuming that they want to carry greater responsibility. It is actually right and proper that the young are allowed to assume certain adult roles without shouldering all the responsibilities that will eventually go with them. They should have the freedom to retreat again into the probationary nature of youth.

Research indicates that the majority of the young are eager for interaction with adults. A sample of over five thousand adolescents was asked whether they would like to discuss their problems with adults and 90% said yes. The caricature of an alienated and rebellious generation, at war with its elders, is dangerous and damaging.

*   *   *

So this attempt to survey adolescence in our society ends with a simple conclusion: that youth is a normal and good period of life. It has certain characteristics that are peculiar to it, but they are best understood against the background of its essential solidarity with other ages. No doubt there are many special stresses on the young person growing up at the end of the twentieth century, but the temptation to sensationalize by exaggeration and caricature must be resisted.

Having said all that, however, can a book written nearly two thousand years ago, in an utterly different culture, still speak immediately and relevantly to our situation today? Has the Bible anything to teach the church about contemporary youth work?

3

The Once and Future Book
The biblical basis for youth work

Youth decay

My wife found herself sitting next to the Bishop as they listened to our church's steel band. Clearly the mix of black and white teenagers playing their animated West Indian rhythms had captured his interest.

'Do they come to church at all?' he asked.

'Oh yes,' she replied, 'and we have a Bible study meeting each week as well.'

'You mean these young people actually read the Bible?' The episcopal eyebrows were raised in astonishment.

The Christian church is not doing well with teenagers. There is quite a bit of work with children, but after thirteen most local churches of whatever denomination (or none) find it hard going. 'Youth decay' sets in. For every church fellowship that has a flourishing group of teenagers in its membership, there are three with virtually no teenagers at all.

So is the whole teenage sub-culture becoming a no-go area for the Christian faith?

There has been no shortage of thought and energy expended in the attempt to reach this age bracket. Teenage popular culture has been analysed and infiltrated by Christians. In the world of music, arts festivals, road shows, magazines, sport and the media, excellent work has been done.

For two decades the attention of the churches has been drawn to the disadvantaged young people of the inner cities. Open youth projects, outreach programmes, skills centres and community work have been organized and run by Christians. The plight of rural young people, with their special problems of isolation and limited resources, has not escaped attention either.

So why, with all the clamour and effort, does the outlook remain so bleak? Are the churches being by-passed now by the Spirit of God, and is he at work in ways and in places that we find hard to perceive? Or does the gospel need to be redefined to make it more relevant to young people conditioned by late twentieth-century Western society?

Or is it just that the Christian faith is actually on an irretrievable decline in the industrial world—a decline most apparent among young people? Has the sea of faith finally ebbed away, and must we now find new ways of defining and speaking about God? Or has our Christian thinking been so infiltrated by secularism and materialism that we are blind to the will of God for his people and to his plans to establish his kingdom?

The challenge

Perhaps some of the answers to the Christian faith's decaying impact on teenagers may lie closer at hand than we think. The fact of a youth-orientated popular culture is so recent, so brash and so dominant, that it is easy to see it as an entirely new phenomenon, posing questions that have never been asked before. It is tempting to believe that the youth decay of the church springs from a failure to understand this new culture, rather than a failure to understand the faith.

But the most serious weakness in the Christian outreach to teenagers today is not a failure to understand our culture. *It is a failure to take the Bible sufficiently seriously*.

There are two imperatives in Christian communication. One is that we take the world we live in seriously, and the other is that we take God's revelation to us in the Bible seriously. If either is missing, the communication will be ineffective.

However, both imperatives can become all-absorbing. We can strive so hard to be relevant and contemporary that we immerse ourselves in our culture to a point where the distinctiveness of the Christian message vanishes. This can happen in Christian social involvement as much as in gospel music. Or, we can be so concerned to be faithful to God's revelation that we forget that the culture of the Bible and the culture of the Western World in the late twentieth century are miles apart. An unbiblical separation is then made between evangelism and social action; or a blanket condemnation is laid over rock music as a medium to communicate the gospel.

However, if we have to err on either side, we must not lose our hold on Christian truth. God has given such a power to the simple message of his love for sinful humanity and of his forgiveness of our sins for the sake of his Son, that our incompetence as communicators is not able to destroy its power to reach non-Christian young people.

That is why some Christian youth work is characterized on the one hand by a massive cultural irrelevance and on the other by an effective changing of human lives. There is other Christian youth work, earnest, sincere and sacrificial, which seems to be popular with young people and to be right on their wavelength, but nevertheless produces few, if any, changed lives, has no permanent effect on the world in which it takes place, and achieves little of eternal significance.

The answer

The cultural distance between the world of the Bible and the world of our own day should not be minimized, but to tell young people about the God who made them and loves them, in a way that they can understand, demands a close attention to what that God has revealed about himself. Here is the foundation for Christian work with teenagers.

The Bible, however, does not contain a systematic theology of youth. There is no mention of the 'teenager' or the 'youth worker'. Adolescents were not regarded as a significant category of society in the ancient world in the way they are today.

Clearly there are problems of 'cultural transposition' in looking back into the Bible to find guidelines for modern youth work. It is necessary to discover the principles that underlay their practices in order to transfer those principles from their culture and apply them to our own culture. We may not wear phylacteries or write texts on our doorposts (Deut 6:8-9), but there may be an important principle that those practices expressed for ancient Judaism which we should not ignore (and for which we must find contemporary applications).

For this search to be successful, it must be expectant and humble. We come to the biblical material expecting to learn from it and willing to learn from it. It must be allowed to speak for itself, however uncomfortable, unfashionable, or alien its voice may sound at first. It is those things which appear least congenial that have most to teach, because they pave the way to new insights and do not merely reinforce our present attitudes and opinions. This is an important principle of study if we are to hear God speaking to us in the Bible. Otherwise we may peer deep into the well of truth, only to see a reflection of our own faces.

It will guard us from despising the youth work of older generations. There can be a dangerous contemporary arrogance which looks down on earlier patterns of youth ministry as though God never guided our predecessors and has reserved his ultimate revelation on this matter for today. Learning Bible verses by heart would be an example of something which our fathers did a lot, but which we tend to neglect as old-fashioned and legalistic.

It will also keep us from making the interpretation of the Bible an intellectual achievement. It is important to study the Bible carefully and diligently, particularly when there is such a large cultural gap between adolescence in the ancient world and adolescence today. But God does not reveal his truth to the learned and conceal it from the simple. Rather the reverse. We set out to master the Bible in order to be mastered by it. The will of God is not so much discerned by an understanding of the 'new hermeneutic', 'dynamic equivalence', or 'redaction criticism', as by our willingness to obey him whatever the cost.

This humble and expectant approach to the Bible will avoid the attitude of detachment, which sees the biblical material as an interesting basis for discussion, but no more than that. Such an attitude resorts to subjectivism ('I think . . . I feel . . . In my experience . . .') at any point where the Bible contradicts previous opinions and prejudices. 'Feeling' may have very little to contribute to the search for God's remedy for the church's youth decay.

So I make no further apology for beginning this search humbly and expectantly in the pages of the Bible.

The God of all ages

While the ancient world knew nothing of the 'teenager', and Eli bringing up Samuel in the Temple must be virtually the only biblical account of a 'youth worker', the Bible has much to say about God's dealings with children and young people. Indeed the Bible is insistent that God is the God of the child. This is particularly striking because children counted for little in ancient society.

With high rates of infant mortality, the child had few rights and low status. Children were a marginalized and disadvantaged social category. When Matthew records Jesus' feeding miracles, he writes, 'And those who ate were about five thousand men, besides women and children' (Mt 14:21), and 'Those who ate were four thousand men, besides women and children' (Mt 15:38), reflecting the social insignificance of the woman and the child.

However, there are some indications of a different attitude. In Leviticus 27 there is a valuation of persons 'vowed to the Lord': a male from twenty years old up to sixty years old was valued at fifty shekels of silver (a woman was valued at thirty), while a male from five years old to twenty years old was worth twenty shekels (and a girl ten). From one month to five years a boy was valued at just five shekels and a girl at three shekels. This suggests that Jewish society did accord a certain status to the child, even if a limited one. Children, and particularly sons, were God's gift to a man and a sign of his blessing:

> Lo, sons are a heritage from the Lord, the fruit of the womb a reward. Like arrows in the hand of a warrior are the sons of one's youth. Happy is the man who has his quiver full of them! He shall not be put to shame when he speaks with his enemies in the gate (Psalm 127:3-5).

Similarly, the 'fatherless' are a category to be protected by law, along with the stranger, the widow and the poor (Exod 22:21-24). Orphans were to be cared for by God's people, in an age which tended to exploit them.

The Old Testament also suggests that an index of what is happening to a society is provided by what is happening to its young. The violent death of small children is an indication of extreme calamity (Nahum 3:10), or the worst of curses on an enemy ('Happy shall be he who takes your little ones and dashes them against the rock!' Ps 137:9). The happiness and well-being of the young are signs that God has visited his people: 'And the streets of the city shall be full of boys and girls playing in its streets' (Zech 8:5); 'Yea, how good and how fair it shall be! Grain shall make the young men flourish, and new wine the maidens' (Zech 9:17).

One of the most abominable of all the Canaanite practices was the worship of Molech, involving children being burnt alive. Any Israelite (or any stranger living in Israel) who offered a child to Molech was to be put to death and to be cut off from among the people (Lev 20:1-5). The very lowest point of degradation for the people of Israel would be when they themselves resorted to eating their own children (Lev 26:29). In the blessings and cursings set before Israel in Deuteronomy 28, the ultimate consequence of rejecting God is that the nation will be afflicted to the point where women will eat their children and even their afterbirths, jealously guarding them from other members of their family. This horrific picture represents the lowest depth to which national life could sink.

The welfare of the young was an important factor in Israelite society because God dealt with the young. He begins his dealings with people even before birth. In Psalm 139 the writer praises God because—

> Thou didst form my inward parts, thou didst knit me together in my mother's womb . . . Thou knowest me right well; my frame was not hidden from thee, when I was being made in secret, intricately wrought in the depths of the earth. Thy eyes beheld my unformed substance; in thy book were written, every one of them, the days that were formed for me, when as yet there was none of them' (Ps 139:13-16).

In certain cases this dealing was specifically related to later ministry. Jeremiah's call to be a prophet began with God telling him, 'Before I formed you in the womb I knew you, and before you were born I consecrated you; I appointed you a prophet to the nations' (Jer 1:5). Samuel was consecrated to God before conception and grew up 'in the presence of the Lord' (1 Sam 2:21), developing 'both in stature and in favour with the Lord and with men' (2:26). Samson was also dedicated before birth and the Lord blessed him in his boyhood (Judg 13:24). Moses was 'beautiful before God' as a baby (Acts 7:20). The angel prophesied of John the Baptist that he would be 'filled with the Holy Spirit, even from his mother's womb' (Lk 1:15). The angel who appeared to the shepherds announced that Jesus, even as an infant a few hours old, was 'Saviour' (Lk 2:11).

Right of access

If the Bible teaches that God can relate to and deals with a person from the moment of conception (and before), it also makes clear that children have their own right of access to God. The disciples tried to prevent overenthusiastic mothers from wasting Jesus' time with blessing their children (Mt 19: 13-15). Their response was typical of their age: it was the parents (and particularly the fathers) who should receive the benefits of Jesus' teaching. Then it could be passed on to the rest of the family at home. But Jesus contradicted this: 'Let the children come to me, and do not hinder them,' he said; 'for to such belongs the kingdom of heaven.' Jesus went against the attitudes and assumptions of his day in asserting the right of children to their own access to God and to their own authentic spiritual experiences.

As far as physical and mental abilities go, there is a growth and development through infancy, childhood, youth and into adulthood, which can be seen as a progression and an improvement. It is not so with the spirit. The child's perception of God may be very different from the adult's, but it is not inferior.

'Thou whose glory above the heavens is chanted by the mouth of babes and infants,' wrote the psalmist (8:1-2), and Jesus quoted that psalm when the chief priests and scribes were indignant at the children crying out, 'Hosanna to the Son of David!' in the temple during his entry into Jerusalem (Mt

21:15-16). When lamenting the reluctance of his contemporaries to believe in him, Jesus declared, 'I thank thee, Father, Lord of heaven and earth, that thou hast hidden these things from the wise and understanding and revealed them to babes; yea, Father, for such was thy gracious will' (Mt 11:25-26).

It would be tempting to limit the word 'babes' *(nēpiois)* to a purely metaphorical sense there, 'the simple, the unsophisticated', were it not for the strong biblical evidence that children do have a special ability to apprehend God. When asked who was greatest in the kingdom of heaven, Jesus brought a child before the disciples and told them that unless they became like children they would never even enter the kingdom of heaven. It was the person who humbled himself like a child who was the greatest in that kingdom (Mt 18:1-4).

A few verses later (18:10) he said, 'See that you do not despise one of these little ones; for I tell you that in heaven their angels always behold the face of my Father who is in heaven.' There are qualities natural to children (which adults must take trouble to imitate) that equip them for an immediate access to God. Their helplessness and dependence are spiritual examples for adults.

Where the ancient world looked down on childhood, Jesus advised his followers not to adopt that attitude. He had 'an affectionate regard for children which was unique among teachers and writers of the ancient world' (R.V.G. Tasker). But this was not mere affection. His attitude was based on theological truth.

This truth is more than a simple glorification of childhood innocence.[26] Authentic spiritual experience is the right of every age. There is not a progression from the inferior and the infantile to the superior and the adult. While we *are* encouraged to be mature in our understanding and our faith, we are also warned not to despise the faith of the young. Indeed, if there is any hierarchy of spiritual experience, Jesus would seem to suggest that the order is the reverse of what we would expect. We are to learn valuable spiritual truths from the young, 'for to such belongs the kingdom of heaven'.[27]

The Bible certainly does not give us any warrant to look down on old age either. It contradicts the ancient world's low estimate of childhood without contradicting their high respect for the old. 'You shall rise up before the hoary head, and honour the face of an old man, and you shall fear your God: I am the Lord' (Lev 19:32). The New Testament says nothing to diminish this injunction.

The God of the Bible is a God of all human ages. The ability of the human spirit to experience its Creator is not limited by the simplicity of childhood, nor by the frailty of old age. So we can be encouraged to extend our search for the Bible's teaching specifically on adolescence knowing that God understands young people, values them, reveals himself to them, and relates to them in a completely appropriate way.

The God of youth

We have already seen from the valuation in Leviticus 27 that there was a probationary period for the young Jew that extended beyond childhood. It was only when they were twenty years old that the full value was put on a man or a woman. Jesus went up with his parents to the temple at Jerusalem when he was twelve (Lk 2:41-52), but it is clear in that passage that the years which followed were a period of development towards full adulthood: 'And he went down with them and came to Nazareth, and was obedient to them; and his mother kept all these things in her heart. And Jesus increased in wisdom and in stature, and in favour with God and man.'

So the Bible does not regard children as adults from their thirteenth birthdays, whatever their official social status. It describes Josiah as 'yet a boy' in the eighth year of his reign, when he was sixteen (2 Chron 34:1-3). There is a category of 'young' men in the Old and New Testaments, distinguished from other age groups: '. . . upon the children in the street, and upon the gatherings of *young men,* also; both husband and wife shall be taken, the old folk and the very aged' (Jer 6:11. See also Joel 2:28). In Titus 2 Paul has injunctions for the 'older men', the 'older women', the 'young women', and the 'younger men' (v.6). In 1 John 2 the author twice addresses the three categories of 'little children', 'fathers', and 'young men' (vv.12-14). In the context these are spiritual categories, but the writer would have derived them from contemporary thinking about human ages. So there was a period of 'youth' in biblical culture.

It may be that there is evidence here for a rather longer probationary period than we have in modern adolescence. Paul was concerned about Timothy's 'youth' in his epistles to his protege (1 Tim 4:12), but from the charge the apostle lays on him Timothy was obviously not an adolescent. For the Romans, the period of adolescence began at seventeen and ended at about twenty-eight. Arndt and Gingrich in their New Testament Greek Lexicon suggest that the word *neanias* (the usual New Testament term for 'youth' or 'young man') covers the period from the twenty-fourth to the fortieth year. But some usages (such as Acts 23:16-22) may indicate that it covers a younger period as well.

Although a young person might enter the world of work and labour in his early teens, he was still allowed a moratorium, a space to develop and grow, before taking on the full responsibilities of mature manhood. How long this period was is not certain, but it would have been equivalent to the experience of adolescence in our own society.[28]

This period was regarded then, as it is today, as a time of probation, of experiment, of trial and error, when a degree of irresponsibility was to be expected, if not commended: 'Rejoice, O young man, in your youth, and let your heart cheer you in the days of your youth; walk in the ways of your heart and the sight of your eyes' (Eccles 11:9). The author goes on to warn of God's judgement and the need to remember our Creator in the days of our youth.

It was also a time for achievement. The Bible records and commends the successes of many young people. In the history books of the Old Testament (particularly the record of David's career in 1 Samuel) the term 'young man' or 'young men' (Hebrew *naar*) was used particularly for those involved in heroic (and often bloodthirsty) feats of arms. The Jericho spies were 'young men' (Josh 6:23). David's own youthfulness was stressed when he slew Goliath (1 Sam 17:33). There is a long list of those who achieved great things in their youth, including Joseph, Samuel, Samson, Joash, Azariah/Uzziah, Josiah, Esther, Daniel, Hananiah and Mishael—a list we could extend perhaps to the New Testament with the lad who provided his lunch for the feeding of the 5,000 in John 6 (v.9), and Paul's nephew who warned the Tribune of the Jewish plot to kill Paul (Acts 23:16-22).[29]

These youthful achievements show that adolescence is a period when great accomplishments and spiritual leadership are possible. Just as the spiritual experience of the young is not to be relegated below adult spirituality, so young men and women are not to wait until adulthood before they can achieve things for God. When Jeremiah said, 'Ah, Lord God! Behold, I do not know how to speak, for I am only a youth,' God replied, 'Do not say, "I am only a youth"; for to all to whom I send you you shall go, and whatever I command you you shall speak' (Jer 1:6-7). God still sends the young to speak for him, just as much as he sends adults.

The church does not do youth and children's work in order to guarantee its own future—to ensure a good supply of future adult believers. It is often said that young people are not 'tomorrow's church' but 'today's church'. The reason why young people are the church of today is not so often stated.

It is not as a patronizing concession to encourage them and make them feel important, nor just because the church is a family and should therefore consist of all ages; but primarily because *God is a God of all ages*. We are only being true to him when we keep young people in the centre of the church's life. Just as distinctions of race or colour or physique or intelligence count for nothing with him, nor do distinctions of age. Every human being is of equal value in his eyes.

So we must not underestimate the spiritual experience and the spiritual potential of the teenager. The Bible suggests that youth is made for heroism. It is the world that insists it is made for pleasure. If we take the Bible seriously, we will look for great spiritual achievements among young people, achievements that will sometimes eclipse those of adults.

Richard Wurmbrand tells the story of a boy in the persecuted Romanian church who arrived one day at the gate of a prison and asked to see the commandant. When he was allowed into the man's office, he said this: 'Today is Mothers' Day and every year on Mothers' Day I buy my mother a bunch of flowers in the market. But last year my mother was put into your prison for being a Christian and she died there. This year I have no one to give my flowers to—so I have brought them here for you, to give to your wife.'

That is the faith that overcomes the world. It is often more powerful in the young than in the old. We should expect a deep spirituality in young people and, if the Bible is a reliable guide, we will not be disappointed. If the Son of God passed through the teenage years (although we know virtually nothing about those years), then there is a pattern of perfect relationship with God appropriate to that age.

*   *   *

As the Bible asserts the high value God puts on young people and the high expectations that he has of their spirituality, it also has much to teach us today about youth evangelism, youth discipling, the church, the family, and patterns of youth work for the local church. These we will consider in turn. The Bishop mentioned at the beginning of this chapter might have found the answer to his question less surprising if he read his Bible with a greater expectation that God does understand the young and has already spoken to them and about them.

4

The Snail on the Sawdust Trail
Adolescent conversion

Sprinkling Christ over social work

In November 1985 a Working Party of the Board of Education of the Church of England presented a report to General Synod on 'Youth Policy in the Church of England'. It included the following:

> *Aims of Christian Youth Work*
> (A) *To support the personal development of young people* so that they will:
> (a) realise their full potential.
> (b) learn to identify their own, and other people's, talents.
> (c) accept that environment, background, etc. will alter the growth of each individual.
> (d) identify, and learn from, situations that might otherwise be seen as 'failures'.
> (e) be supported in their questioning of the accepted values of society.
> (f) be encouraged to identify and welcome the spiritual, social, political and cultural development of their personalities.

(B) *To work within a partnership* of mutual respect with other agencies concerned with the development of young people.

It also had a 'Statement of Intent towards Young People (from anyone engaging in Christian youth work)':

(a) I believe that we are all children of God.

(b) I am prepared to respond to what *you* tell me you *want,* not just to tell you what *I* think you *need.*

(c) I believe that this will help to create an atmosphere where you can begin to take responsibility for your own, and other people's, lives.

(d) I accept that *I* have responsibility for the consequences of the initiatives that I make to *you.*

This humble and self-effacing approach, focusing so strongly on the young people themselves, deserves respect. But it is not based on a Christian understanding of man. Christ does not teach us to support the personal development of young people so that they may realize their full potential. We are instead to call them to repentance and faith, because only in that way can they begin to realize their full potential.

General Synod rejected the report (which is in itself a rare occurrence).

The first aim of Christian youth work must be to present a young person with the claims of Jesus Christ.[30] It is only by an encounter with the living God that a young person's deepest needs can be met.

Those who represent the Church to youth will have betrayed their trust if the young people who pass through their hands have not been confronted with the Person of the living Christ, and so brought to the point of decision whether or no they will accept him as Saviour and King, and serve him in the fellowship of his Church (*Towards The Conversion of England* 1945).

Jesus teaches that a man's worst problems lie within his own heart (Mk 7:23). But the solution to those problems does not lie within. They have destroyed a relationship with God that only God can restore. It is an understanding and a trust in what God did for us through the incarnation, crucifixion and resurrection of his Son that sets us free to relate to him. Only in that relationship can a young person—or anyone else—find real freedom and fulfilment. Jesus made the choice clear, and did not conceal the consequences of rejecting God's offer.

If any man would come after me, let him deny himself and take up his cross and follow me. For whoever would save his life will lose it; and whoever loses his life for my sake and the gospel's will save it. For what does it profit a man, to gain the whole world and forfeit his life? For what can a man give in return for his life? For whoever is ashamed of me and of my words in this adulterous and sinful generation, of him will the Son of man also be ashamed, when he comes in the glory of his Father with the holy angels (Mk 8:34-38).

Youth work is not 'Christian' if it is not true to Jesus Christ in facing young people with this gospel and warning them of the consequences of not accepting it. It is this message that distinguishes Christian youth work from secular youth work. If we abandon it, we are discarding the most important contribution that we as Christians can make.

British society was probably never 'Christian' in any realistic sense. Certainly today the majority of the population do not live their lives with any reference to the lordship of Jesus Christ. The Christian response to a non-Christian (or post-Christian) society is to challenge individuals to face Christ's claims. This even comes before the regeneration of the society itself. If Christianity has influenced the history of the human race at all, it has been primarily because of the conversion of individuals. God does not start anywhere else with mankind.

Of course, renewed individuals are called to challenge the presuppositions and structures of society. It is not a choice between the regeneration of individuals or the changing of society. Both must go together. But whenever Christianity has failed to convert individuals, it has quickly ceased to have any long-term effects upon the culture.

So Christian youth work will focus on the individual, but it is not individualistic. The 'cult of self-actualization' or the 'discovery of personhood' can sound quite Christian. Christianity *does* teach the dignity and freedom of the individual. We are each of great value, a value quite independent of our looks, our abilities, our achievements, our popularity, even our own estimates of ourselves.

But Christianity does not encourage a quest to find our true 'self'. The idea of the real inner 'me', whom I need to recognize, acknowledge, affirm and release to be myself, is not Christian at all. It is a Greek idea which makes us out to be onions: if we peel off enough skins, eventually we will discover the real identity within. But what if, when we finally discard the last skin, there is no one home?

Our cultural emphasis on self-authentication—'I did it my way', 'I've gotta be me'—is summarized in the Bible by a single short word: sin. There is not a real, true self lurking within young people which we should be helping them to discover. They discover their real selves by submission to God, who first shaped them within the womb and who remakes them in Christ into the individuals they were really meant to be. We do not *find* ourselves; we are *made* ourselves by God.

That is the Christian approach to the search for personal identity. The individual discovers his own identity as he chooses to enter a relationship with his Maker. As he receives God's Spirit and has God's law written upon his heart, so he finds out who he is. The biblical injunction is not to 'find' myself, but to 'lose' myself (Mk 8:35).[31]

A biblical balance

We see this demonstrated by the delicate balance the Bible maintains between the individual and the community. The solidarity of the individual with his family, his tribe and his nation is stressed. The covenant with Abraham, although made with an individual, is a covenant with the nation:

> I will establish my covenant between me and you and your descendants after you throughout their generations for an ever-lasting covenant . . . and I will give to you . . . all the land of Canaan (Gen 17:7-8).

This was a meaningless promise, in terms of the agreement with Abraham as an individual, seeing its fulfilment was several centuries away. But Abraham would live on in his descendants, and his descendants were already present in him.

This helps to explain verses which seem particularly hard for us, such as God declaring to Moses that he would visit 'the iniquity of the fathers upon the children and the children's children, to the third and fourth generation' (Exod 34:7). There would have been no discrepancy or discord in the minds of the Israelites between the beautiful early verses of Psalm 137, lamenting the captivity in Babylon— 'By the waters of Babylon, there we sat down and wept, when we remembered Zion'—and the fearful final verse: 'Happy shall he be who takes your little ones and dashes them against the rock!' We find such sentiments horrific, but for Israel to wish for the destruction of their enemies, the Babylonians, and to leave the Babylonian children to live on, would be a contradiction, for the Babylonians still lived in their children.

This corporate dimension to all human life is present in the New Testament as well. Paul and Silas had no hesitation in telling the Philippian jailer that if *he* believed in the Lord Jesus he would be saved *with* his household (Acts 16).

We have lost our sense of this corporate involvement with one another, our sense of identity with our families and our nation. It is not that the Bible is odd in its sense of communal solidarity, but that we are odd in our overdeveloped individualism. This has many applications to youth ministry which we will need to consider in time. But first we must look at the other side of the coin.

There is also a clear case for individual responsibility throughout the Bible. Christian youth work must start with the individual, although it cannot end there.

The balance is apparent in the covenant God made with the house of David. When David planned to build the temple, the prophet Nathan was sent to him by God to say:

> When your days are fulfilled and you lie down with your fathers, I will raise up your offspring after you, who shall come forth from your body, and I will establish his kingdom. . . . I will establish the throne of his kingdom for ever. . . . I will not take my steadfast love from him, as I took it from Saul, whom I put away from before you. And your house and your kingdom shall be made sure for ever before me; your throne shall be established for ever (2 Sam 7:12-16).

But, when God later spoke to Solomon about the building of the Temple, it was clear that the promise to David had not removed from Solomon his own freedom and individuality:

> Now the word of the Lord came to Solomon, 'Concerning this house which you are building, *if* you will walk in my statutes and obey my ordinances and keep all my commandments and walk in them, *then* I will establish my word with you, which I spoke to David your father (1 Kings 6:11-13).

The conditional promise never removed the freedom of the following generations. They were still free to reject (by refusing to obey God's commands) what God had promised to their fathers. At the dedication of the Temple, it was clear that Solomon had understood the conditions. He specifically reminded God of the words of his promise to David—'There shall never fail you a man before me to sit upon the throne of Israel, *if only* your sons take heed to their way, to walk before me, as you have walked before me' (1 Kings 8:25. See also Psalm 89:29-39).

It would seem that the children did not have to opt into the covenant, but they were never counted in against their choice. Here is the delicate balance between corporate solidarity, whereby God deals with a whole community through the generations, and individual responsibility, where each man must answer for his own sin. As they emerge into adulthood, we should be calling teenagers to make their own choice and to take responsibility for their own spiritual lives.

New covenant

The new covenant stresses individual accountability and personal relationship. The context of the well-known passage about the new covenant in Jeremiah 31 (twice quoted in the epistle to the Hebrews) highlights this shift in emphasis:

> In those days they shall no longer say: 'The fathers have eaten sour grapes, and the children's teeth are set on edge.' But every one shall die for his own sin; each man who eats sour grapes, his teeth shall be set on edge. Behold, the days are coming, says the Lord, when I will make a new covenant with the house of Israel . . . No longer shall each man teach his neighbour and each his brother, saying, 'Know the Lord,' for they shall all know me, from the least of them to the greatest, says the Lord; for I will forgive their iniquity, and I will remember their sin no more (Jer 31:29-34).

The contrast is between an old covenant, which dealt with the whole people of God corporately, and a new covenant, under which individuals will experience a personal relationship with God through the forgiveness of sins. Religious experience will no longer be mediated through the whole people—each man teaching his neighbour, saying, 'Know the Lord,' but every individual 'from the least of them to the greatest' will have his own experience of God, because he will have God's law written within him, written upon his heart.

The same vision inspired Joel:

> And it shall come to pass afterward, that I will pour out my spirit

on all flesh; your sons and your daughters shall prophesy, your old men shall dream dreams, and your young men shall see visions. Even upon the menservants and maidservants in those days, I will pour out my spirit (Joel 2:28-29).

No longer will there be an 'elite' of the Spirit—prophets, priests and kings, who experienced God's Spirit on behalf of the nation—but he would now become the property of all people, so that the individual might have a personal experience of God, and so discover his individual identity.

This individualism is confirmed by Jesus' warning that family unity will sometimes be shattered by faith in him (Mt 10:35-36; Lk 12:52; 21:16). The parable of the prodigal son focuses on a relationship of free individuals, and in its context in Luke 19 (where it is preceded by the parables of the lost sheep and the lost coin) highlights the importance of the individual to God: 'Just so, I tell you, there will be more joy in heaven over one sinner who repents than over ninety-nine righteous persons who need no repentence' (Lk 15:7).

We have already considered how his teaching on childhood and youth hinged on the right of every individual of whatever age to immediate access to God, contradicting the assumptions of the ancient world about childhood. When questioned about a man blind from birth (Jn 9:1-3), Jesus denied the possibility that his blindness could be attributed to his parents' sin, again rejecting his contemporaries' assumptions about corporate solidarity.

We need to apply this Bible teaching to the adolescent quest for identity. The individual is given his identity by commitment to, and relationship with, God. It is by decision and by commitment that individual identity is determined. The adolescent does not need to travel to the East to 'find himself', as was so fashionable in the 60s and 70s. There is no discovery of identity to be made by inward contemplation or soul-searching. By submission to God the individual brings himself to the point where he can learn from God, and God can bring him into reality.

It was only when David's sons committed themselves to walk before God as David had walked before God, that the covenant became a reality for them. They appropriated for themselves that relationship which allowed God to do for them all the good he had promised their forefather. That was the moment at which they began to realize their full potential.

When a young person wants to step out of the crowd, to be 'himself' rather than just another member of a group, that is the moment at which God can meet him. It is only in relationship to God that he can find his full individuality. That relationship is discovered by exercising the will to choose: to choose to make personal a general and corporate offer from the Creator. This choice enables a person to grow up. Man finds his identity by exercising choice.

Back to the old rugged cross

It is this choice that Christian youth work will be offering young people, and the cross of Christ will always be at the centre of it. The cross challenges young people as individuals to choose. It shows them the enormous love that God has for them and the very high price he was prepared to pay to forgive them—'But God shows his love for us in that while we were yet sinners Christ died for us' (Rom 5:8).

The crisis of self-esteem that is such a common experience in adolescence is not satisfied by repeated and well-meaning assurances like: 'You're not nearly as bad as you think you are.' Every time a friend says that to a depressed young person, a little voice inside wants to say, 'If only you knew me, you'd know I am really far worse.'

The cross of Jesus provides a quite different answer. It says, 'Actually, you know, you are much worse than you think you are—so bad that Jesus had to die an appalling death to bear the dreadful separation that your evil has made between you and God. But God loves you so much, just as you are here and now, that he sent Jesus to die that death for you. And

Jesus *has done* that. God values you that much. And now he offers you new life for Jesus' sake.'

The cross offers new life. But it also makes clear the starkness of the choice. When Jesus invited his followers to take up their cross and follow him, they would have been in no doubt at all as to what he meant. If you saw someone carrying a cross in first-century Palestine, you did not see that person again. He was on a one-way journey to the grave. Jesus meant the end of one sort of self-centred life and the start of a completely different life. So Paul wrote:

> I have been crucified with Christ; it is no longer I who live, but Christ who lives in me; and the life I now live in the flesh I live by faith in the Son of God, who loved me and gave himself for me (Gal 2:20).

So the cross is a good anchor point in Christian youth work. It will guard against it becoming secular youth work with a nominal religious veneer. Christian youth work is not just youth work with an extra spiritual dimension to it: doing what the Youth Service does, but doing it rather worse because of a lack of funds, and pushing in a 'God slot' because it is being held on church premises. Christian youth work is done first and foremost in obedience to Christ—who told us to make disciples of all nations, and died on the cross so that this might be possible.

It will also guard against the temptation to change the gospel when we find that results do not come easily. If Christian youth work aims at the conversion of the individual, and individuals do not get converted, then questions are bound to arise. It is right that they should. But we have already been warned that the message we proclaim will be neither sensational nor popular. 'For Jews demand signs and Greeks seek wisdom,' wrote Paul, 'but we preach Christ crucified, a stumbling block to Jews and folly to Gentiles' (1 Cor 1:22-23).

The message of the cross will not be popular. It will not normally provoke a massive response. It is right that we should regularly examine our message to check that we have not added anything unnecessary to it. There may be cultural accretions which need to be shed. Sometimes it is not the gospel that is being rejected, but the class, educational and cultural overtones that we have laid upon it. It is essential that these are regularly and ruthlessly removed.

For example, we like to grade sin so that some sins are much more evil than others. Child abuse would be high up on the list today, but hypocrisy would be way down, and material self-improvement scarcely gets on to the list at all. Such hierarchies of sin are derived from our culture, not from our Bibles. They need frequent re-examination.

The final test must be whether our gospel is true to God's revealed will in the Bible, not whether it is cutting ice with contemporary society. We can only redefine the gospel to make it truer to the work and teaching of Jesus. Once we start redefining it to make it more relevant today, or to certain parts of society, we have begun a dangerous journey. History is littered with examples of those who have thought to improve on the gospel. The story may be apocryphal, but the French statesman Talleyrand gave a delightful answer to his friend, Lepeaux, who had founded a religion to improve on Christianity. He complained about his lack of success and Talleyrand replied, 'There is one plan you might at least try: why not be crucified and then rise again on the third day?'

Evangelism is central to Christian youth work and that means the cross must be central. But a commitment to evangelism and proclaiming the cross will need to be seasoned with a mature understanding of young people and the emotional pressures of adolescence.[32]

A people obsessed by power

'I want everyone to bow their heads and close their eyes. No one is to look. If God has spoken to you tonight . . . and you want to respond to what he has been saying, please raise your hand to God. No one will be looking. This is just between you and him. Just raise your hand to tell him you are willing to do what he wants you to.'

Even as the young evangelist spoke, it struck me that there was one person in the hall that evening who did not need anyone to raise their hands to indicate the state of their hearts. God knew exactly who was responding and who was not. The raised hands were not for his benefit.

Had all eyes been open and every head up, the gesture would have been a public profession of faith—a helpful first step, perhaps, to confessing Christ with their lips. Then it would have been for the benefit of those responding. But the speaker insisted that every head remained bowed and every eye closed. It was his first remark to me after the meeting that revealed the real purpose of the raised hands: 'Mark, did you see the response?'

It was for his benefit that those young people had raised their hands. He had been watching (and he had expected me to be watching), because he needed the encouragement of seeing that the gospel worked.

This small incident highlights the weakness of much youth evangelism. We judge it by standards of success or failure, and not by its obedience to God's will. We have allowed ourselves to become besotted with the power images of contemporary youth culture.

For example, there is an emphasis on gathering together large numbers, so that 'they can see that they are not alone'. There is an emphasis on 'big name' speakers and the testimonies of well-known individuals, so that the young can see that even the greater, the famous and the powerful believe. There is an emphasis on the visible response of large numbers, so that we reverse Paul's dictum that 'we walk by faith and not by sight', and we encourage the young to trust the big battalions rather than the cross of Christ. There is an emphasis on immediacy, excitement, challenge and enthusiasm, so that the answer to doubt is presented as constant exhortation to greater emotional commitment. There is an emphasis on the discipleship of the big event, so that the normal teenage testimony is one of crisis rather than growth.[33]

This shallow pattern of evangelism is often coupled with a disdain for the local church. The outward image of the local church will frequently be caricatured and pilloried by youth speakers, as a way of ingratiating their message to their hearers. In this way young people are encouraged to adopt a superior and judgemental attitude to the church, not just in its local denominational manifestation, but as the totality of the adult community of faith. They start to see their job as one of changing the church, not loving it and belonging to it.

We will return to this in chapter seven, and we will see there that the widespread dissatisfaction among young people with traditional patterns of Christianity may be a very welcome development. But evangelism that does not take the doctrine of the church seriously will do considerable damage in the long run, because conversion is not just an individual thing. It must have a strong corporate dimension to it.

The gospel is certainly immediate, exciting and challenging, but this must be tempered with the stark and sober realism of the choice before a young person. The excitement is much more acceptable than the starkness in our age which believes this is what young people want. We must achieve a biblical balance—not neglecting the thrills, but bringing the spills into the open as well. There is no 'Christianity without tears'.

The invitation to wisdom

This is emphasized by the interesting distinction between the Bible's teaching about children and its teaching about young people.

With the *child* there is an emphasis on firm teaching and discipline:

> Train up a child in the way he should go, and when he is old he will not depart from it (Prov 22:6).

> Folly is bound up in the heart of a child, but the rod of discipline drives it far from him (Prov 22:15).

> Do not withhold discipline from a child; if you beat him with a rod, he will not die. If you beat him with a rod you will save his life from Sheol (Prov 23:13-14).

But with the *young person* there is the invitation to wisdom, frequently offered in the book of Proverbs:

> Hear, O sons, a father's instruction, and be attentive, that you may gain insight; for I give you good precepts: do not forsake my teaching. When I was a son with my father, tender, the only one in the sight of my mother, he taught me, and said to me, 'Let your heart hold fast my words; keep my commandments, and live; do not forget, and do not turn away from the words of my mouth. Get wisdom; get insight. Do not forsake her, and she will keep you; love her, and she will guard you. The beginning of wisdom is this: Get wisdom, and whatever you get, get insight' (Prov 4:1-7).

The approach is open; various ways lie before the young person on the threshold of adult life. There are rival offers for his allegiance. It may be the company of evil men (Prov 1:10-19), or the lure of the seductress (Prov 5 and 7). But against these wisdom makes her appeal:

> Wisdom cries aloud in the street; in the markets she raises her voice; on the top of the walls she cries out; at the entrance of the city gates she speaks: 'How long, O simple ones, will you love being simple? How long will scoffers delight in their scoffing and fools hate knowledge? Give heed to my reproof; behold, I will pour out my thoughts to you; I will make my words known to you' (Prov 1:20-23).

The tone is quite different from the Bible's instructions to children—'Children, obey your parents in the Lord, for this is right' (Eph 6:1); 'Children, obey your parents in everything, for this pleases the Lord' (Col 3:20). There is a recognition of the increasing independence of adolescents, of their right to make up their own minds, and of their dignity in exercising freedom of choice as beings made in God's image. To be adult is to make your own choices. The wisdom literature of the Bible presents the young with the fundamental choices of life and pleads with them to choose correctly.

The strong emphasis on 'wisdom' is not to be mistaken for the quest for intellectual achievement. Academic success is one of the false gods of modern Western society. Worship of the intellect is quite different from the way of wisdom urged on us in the book of Proverbs. This wisdom involves accepting and appropriating the older generation's advice: 'A wise son hears his father's instruction, but a scoffer does not listen to rebuke' (Prov 13:1).

It is not adorned to make it particularly attractive to the young. The starkness of the choice is made abundantly clear: hard work, moral uprightness, discipline, humility, suffering, faithfulness, maturity and discretion are all stressed. But wisdom is also God's gift. The young are not invited to achieve it, but to choose it, to seek it:

> Yes, if you cry out for insight and raise your voice for understanding, if you seek it like silver and search for it as for hidden treasures; then you will understand the fear of the Lord and find the knowledge of God. For the Lord gives wisdom (Prov 2:3-6).

It was God who made Daniel and his three colleagues wise (Dan 1:17). It is God who by the cross has reversed the wisdom of the world (1 Cor 1:22-25), and now reveals an eternal wisdom through his Spirit (1 Cor 2:6-10).

The Bible respects youth's aspiration to adulthood and presents the young with a realistic choice. There is no distortion to tip the balance unfairly in one direction. There is a deep respect for the dignity and freedom of the young person. Nothing is concealed. There is no small print, no hidden clauses, but the urgency of the plea is unmistakable: 'My son, give me your heart, and let your eyes observe my ways' (Prov 23:26). It is a life-or-death choice upon which every person's ultimate happiness depends.

There is much here to apply directly to modern youth evangelism. Is our evangelism as honest and as free from deceit? Do we show the same respect for the freedom and dignity of the teenager? Do we make the choice as clear and as urgent? Are we sometimes guilty, not of asking too much, but of asking too little of teenagers and so selling them and God short? Are we clear that our appeal springs out of the nature and mind of God, rather than culturally-conditioned motives to do with success? Is our offer really the wisdom which 'the Lord created . . . at the beginning of his work, the first of his acts of old' (Prov 8:22), a wisdom which has made Christ crucified 'the power of God and the wisdom of God' (1 Cor 1:24)? The cross lies at the centre of this wisdom and must therefore also be the centre of our evangelism.

Sheep fed on lollipops

We must have a sensitive concern for the young people that we work with, so that we are not tempted to deceive them in any way. We will want to teach them the whole counsel of God with our lives and with our lips.

> Jesus wept? Jesus weeps. He weeps over sheep fed on lollipops . . . He weeps over poor, deceived young people who are falsely taught by enthusiastic preachers that an instant, subjective experience at a special conference will solve all their problems and give them a zippy, automatic, Christian joy for the rest of their lives. Garbage! Lying and devilish garbage—that leads young Christians to despair, to frustration, and to the terrible sense that if things go wrong, God has abandoned them or they have failed (John White).[34]

Our theology must be sufficiently mature to cope with evangelism that fails to get immediate results. In some Christian writing it would appear that evangelism never fails, that it cannot fail. So exaggeration and distortion creep in. Tentative enquirers become converts. Numbers are rounded up. Sensational results are triumphantly proclaimed. We must equip our young people with a theology that can cope with failure.

God does not need statistics to prove his power to save young people. Nor is our own faith built up by that attitude. All too often it is undermined when we compare our first-hand experience of evangelism with the way it is reported in the Christian press. Nor is the non-Christian world impressed with what is too evidently propaganda.

We must take to heart the parable of the sower (Mk 4:1-20). It was the seed which fell on rocky soil that sprang up with joy. How many of those who hurry to the front at an evangelistic rally are in that category? We must beware of equating the act of 'coming forward' with conversion.

We must beware of working with young people in order to meet our own emotional needs. Some evangelistic pro-grammes for the young insist on a visible response to the gospel, not for the sake of the young people themselves, but for the sake of the leaders who need encouragement in their own ministry.

We must not rob the cross of its power. God is able to save by many or by few. His redemptive work has carried on down the ages. It is not thwarted by the failure of human agencies. He still calls young people to himself through the simple message of forgiveness for Jesus' sake: that they can stop trying to please God in order to earn forgiveness from him, and start rejoicing in the fact that he is already pleased with them just as they are, because Jesus has already paid the price for that forgiveness. 'For Christ also died for sins once for all, the righteous for the unrighteous, that he might bring us to God' (1 Pet 3:18). It is a message that releases supernatural power into the individual to start to transform him, and through him to start to transform his world.

This message is going to continue to change human lives, whether we can see it happening, and count it, or not. Young people are particularly open to considering it. Of the 14,857 enquirers who came forward at the Luis Palau Mission to London in 1984, 65% were aged between twelve and twenty-five (23% of the general population fall in that age range). This susceptibility to spiritual enquiry should make us particularly careful in our definition of adolescent conversion.

Decisions, decisions!

The number of different models used in the New Testament to describe the character of God's salvation (legal justification, new birth, adoption into a family, washing, from death to life, liberation, accepting lordship, indwelling of God, sacrificial atonement, from darkness to light, turning round, etc.) serves to remind us of the limitations of our own ability to understand God's dealings with man. We are not going to find a clear and total explanation of adolescent conversion.

However, a balance is revealed between God's part in regenerating us and our part in receiving and believing: 'To all who received him, who believed in his name, he gave power to become children of God; who were born, not of blood nor of the will of the flesh nor of the will of man, but of God' (Jn 1:12-13). A man cannot will himself to be born. Only God can will it. But God does not do so against the man's will. Much theological ink has been spilt over this point (of the freedom of the human will), and it would not be appropriate to discuss it here, but we must make a distinction between God's action and man's response.

The inward spiritual work of regeneration is done by God out of sight. It is an eternal act which cannot be overthrown. The outward profession of conversion is visible and may or may not be genuine. It may come and go, even in an adult. For the teenager this outward profession of conversion presents some particular problems.

The teenager stands between childhood and adulthood. The child is not a free agent. She can only commit to God as much of her time, energy, property, will-power and emotions as she herself is in control of. As she develops greater autonomy and responsibility, so she has to develop a more complete commitment to God. The anomaly of the teenager, or even the adult, trying to live her life with a Sunday School faith is all too familiar.

In some ways the individual who first encounters Christ as an adult has an easier path to tread. Her faith does not have to keep in step with the traumatic upheavals of puberty and adolescence as it first grows and develops. Christians working with children have rightly felt that it is unwise to use highly subjective language about conversion ('Is Jesus real to you?' is a dangerously difficult question for a child to have to answer) and have often preferred to talk about 'following Jesus' rather than 'receiving Jesus'. They also know the dangers of asking a child for an emotionally drastic step of commitment, which makes it very hard for that child to cope with failure and defeat later. How many adults there are who once made some great step of faith as a child and, because it did not 'work', will have nothing more to do with Christ!

Adolescence must be handled just as sensitively. As youth workers we proclaim Christ to our young people and we pray that God will convert them, but we have to direct our attention to the outward and visible human response. On his side, God deals with young people in a way that is entirely appropriate to their age and development (as we saw in chapter three). We do not know exactly what that means for the inward work of regeneration—there is no material in the Bible that gives us specific insight into this—but we must work out what it means for the outward work of conversion.

The young person needs psychological space in which to develop. We need to remember what it was like to be a teenager. The most powerful convictions of one week may have blurred and dimmed by the next. Our most deeply committed young people at one meeting may seem to be distinctly cool at another. As a young person struggles to discover his own identity, we must be very sensitive about confusing that search by trying to hang adult labels upon him, which may satisfy us but are unhelpful to him. On the one hand we believe passionately that his fundamental need is for a personal experience of the living God, but on the other hand we treat him with all the love and sensitivity and maturity that the living God inspires in us.

This may mean allowing a young person to leave a youth fellowship. God allowed his first child, Adam, to disobey him. He did not change the rules when he saw that he was about to eat the forbidden fruit. The prodigal son was given his share of the property and allowed to leave the family home. We are less than biblical when we exert great emotional pressure to keep a young person in a fellowship. Perhaps we do it more because we ourselves cannot live with the prospect of failure, than because we are concerned to obey God and to love and respect the individual.

We will need to help our young people constantly to update their faith, to find appropriate expression for it as their own stage of life changes. We will be cautious to respect their vulnerability to emotional pressure. The big event and the large crowd can communicate a message that its organizers never intended. The fourteen-year-old girl, whose first steady relationship with a boyfriend has just ended, may be making a completely genuine response to the offer of the friendship of Jesus, but the wise youth worker will take it with a pinch of gently-loving salt. He will try to guard her against making a drastic commitment that was never genuine in the first place, and from which she can only later extricate herself by abandoning all contact with the Christian faith.

We will want to reflect on what we are doing when we apply adult methods of evangelism to young people. A stereotyped adult model of conversion does not fit them, so it is unlikely that adult methods of evangelism will meet their needs, but the statistics show very clearly that crusade-style evangelism *will* prove to be a youth event. The organizers have no excuse for surprise when an age-analysis shows that a very high percentage of those who came forward were teenagers. (54% of all Mission England enquirers were eighteen or under—and half of those were girls aged between eleven and eighteen.) Therefore, there must be careful thought given to adequate youth nurture and follow-up at such events.

It must be recognized that the conversion of a young person is not just an individual crisis (a personal decision on a particular evening at a particular meeting). It also has a gradual and a corporate dimension to it. Some youth workers like to think in terms of a 'four-year conversion', an extended process in the life of a young person in which he comes from darkness to light. At some point, perhaps at the beginning, perhaps at the end, God regenerates that person. We have no infallible insight into when that may be in any individual case. At some point the young person himself professes conversion. That may or may not coincide with God's work of regeneration. But along the way these things happen.

It is the task of the youth leader to care prayerfully for the young person through all those years. In one sense the call to conversion never ends in the life of the believer. The Holy Spirit will continue to lay claim to fresh areas of our lives throughout our earthly pilgrimage. In another sense there is only one moment in which each individual passes from death to life, as God through his Spirit enters our hearts.

It is more helpful to young people to view conversion in the light of this gradual process, than to put too much emphasis on the crisis decision. The challenge to decide must be faithfully made—the cross demands that—but we must be reluctant to hang 'saved' or 'unsaved' labels too hastily around our young people's necks. It is sometimes easier (and more helpful) to ask the question: 'Is he or she spiritually hungry?' or: 'Which way is he or she facing at the moment?' than to ask the question: 'Is he or she saved?' We are desperate for the answer to the latter question (and rightly so), but God does not always trust us with it. We may have to persevere with the faithful work of an under-shepherd and leave the eventual outcome of the matter to him.

If it is a gradual process, it is also a corporate one. The church, whether we like it or not, is a part of the gospel. God calls us into community. This is specially relevant to the teenager. It is notoriously hard for a young person under sixteen to hold an independent set of beliefs. He or she needs to be part of a tribe.[35]

We put unknown pressures on the forming personality if we expect a young person to reject identification with other teenagers for the sake of Christ. Somehow or other we must provide a community of faith into which the young person can move. In a frontier situation, this may be the foremost obstacle to evangelism. It may be necessary to look across denominational boundaries, across social and cultural barriers, even across a considerable geographical distance, but some sort of acceptable Christian fellowship must be found. If we neglect this corporate aspect of adolescent conversion, we will seriously jeopardize our youth evangelism.

The test is time

Young people need time and space as they grow up. They need to be protected from the evangelist or the youth worker who sees them as statistics. They are eager to get up out of their seats and come down to the front at rallies and crusades, but, when they do, they need to meet adults with mature theology and a sympathetic understanding of youth. They must be allowed to take as much time as they need to make their own genuine response to God. They should hit the sawdust trail at their own pace.

Youth leaders need great maturity. Emerson said that 'the lesson of life is to believe what the years and centuries say against the hours'. It is certainly the lesson of youth work to believe what the years say against the weeks. All too familiar are the mushroom youth fellowships that spring up and flourish, only to wither and vanish again in a year or two. Many adult Christians today look back on a flourishing youth fellowship during their teenage years and wonder what has become of most of their contemporaries. We will look at this phenomenon again in a later chapter.

Youth workers need great wisdom. Francis Bacon observed that all that is weighty in history sinks to the bottom of the river where it cannot be seen, while straw and stubble rise to the top. So it is in youth work. We must look beneath the surface. The wise worker is not over-impressed by numbers, by chorus singing, by the 'atmosphere' of a youth meeting, or by young people's own estimates of their spiritual maturity. He or she will pray for that God-given gift of discernment to see deeper into their lives and into their real spiritual needs.

Looking into a river, you may have to make a conscious effort to cut out the surface reflection in order to see the depths. Sometimes in youth work it is necessary deliberately to put surface impressions on one side in order to perceive real spiritual needs. If we love the young people we work with, we will pray for the ability to see below their surfaces. We will not be content to take them at face value.

As we have considered this picture of adolescent conversion, we have drawn some conclusions for youth evangelism along the way, but the main question remains: how then is the gospel best communicated to young people? Answering that question will raise wider issues than just evangelism, so I will deal with it in a separate chapter. In particular we will see that the line between evangelizing (outreach) and discipling (teaching) is far from clear.

5

Faith-to-Faith Communication
Evangelizing and discipling young people (i)

A problem as old as the hills

'Can a truly contemporary man not be an atheist?' asked John Robinson in *Honest to God* (1963). He was expressing a widespread feeling that it is much harder to believe today than it was in previous ages. Somehow we feel it is more difficult to communicate Christianity to a modern person than it would have been to communicate it to a Victorian.

It is not an impression that bears close examination. The problem of passing the faith from one generation to another has always tested the people of God. It is dealt with at length in the Bible. It is in fact one of the major themes of the Old Testament.

We find there not only a recognition of the problem, but also powerful teaching on how to communicate faith effectively. It is teaching that speaks directly to our situation today, thousands of years later. We tend to overlook what it is saying because we expect to have to transfer Old Testament teaching from its cultural setting to our own. That task does need doing, but far less than many would lead us to believe. In fact, the Old Testament starts right where we are in this matter.

The spiritual realities of one generation will often be remote and unreal to their sons:

> And the people served the Lord all the days of Joshua, and all the days of the elders who outlived Joshua, who had seen all the great work which the Lord had done for Israel. . . . And all that generation also were gathered to their fathers; and there arose another generation after them, who did not know the Lord or the work which he had done for Israel (Judg 2:7-10).

The same tale is repeated many times. God would act powerfully at one stage in the nation's history, but memories quickly grew dim and the reality of faith faded as a new generation arose.

From the outset this danger had been taken into account. The religious life of the Israelites was impregnated with a concern to communicate faith effectively from one generation to the next. The purpose of circumcision was that it should be a sign of the covenant to future generations; so that at eight days old the Israelite male received in his body a powerful and permanent communication about the faith from the previous generation (Gen 17:9-14).

The whole religious life of Israel was structured to elicit enquiry from the young. The various religious customs and festivals that the Jews were to keep in Canaan were not merely quaint reminders of their religious past. Nor were they just teaching opportunities for a father to lecture his children on the faith. They were vivid enactments of the past that were certain to cause the young to ask questions. 'And when your children say to you, "What do you mean by this service?" you shall say, "It is the sacrifice of the Lord's passover"' (Exod 12:26-27).

Animal sacrifice, particularly of a lamb which had been living with the family for a week, would inevitably provoke strident questioning from younger members of the family. Imagine having the rabbit 'put to sleep' to celebrate some major holiday today. The vividness of the communication cannot be denied.

The sacrifice (or redemption) of first-born male animals and the redemption of every first-born son would prompt the same response:

> And when in time to come your son asks you, 'What does this mean?' you shall say to him, 'By strength of hand the Lord brought us out of Egypt, from the house of bondage. For when Pharaoh stubbornly refused to let us go, the Lord slew all the first-born in the land of Egypt, both the first-born of man and the first-born of cattle. Therefore I sacrifice to the Lord all the males that first open the womb; but all the first-born of my sons I redeem' (Exod 13:14-15).

The Feast of Booths was equally-well designed to provoke enquiry (Deut 31:10-13), and there are other examples in Joshua 4:6, 21 and Joshua 22:24.

The emphasis falls, not on the father's teaching, but on the son's questioning and then the father's replying. This was the purpose of the nation's religious practices: 'When your son asks you in time to come, "What is the meaning of the testimonies and the statutes and the ordinances which the Lord our God has commanded you?" *then* you shall say to your son . . .' (Deut 6:20-21).

Throughout the Torah (the Law) there is this passionate concern that the next generation should know the Lord. They saw the problem of 'youth decay' and were concerned to prevent it right from the start:

> Only take heed, and keep yourselves diligently, lest you forget the things which your eyes have seen, and lest they depart from your heart all the days of your life; make them known to your children and your children's children . . . that they may teach their children so (Deut 4:9-10).

When we realize how deeply this determination affected the religious life of Israel, we are challenged to examine the life of our own churches. Do they show as great a desire to communicate the faith to the younger generation in a living way? We may think that circumcision and animal sacrifice are quaint and barbaric, but have we found equally vivid means of communication? Can we really say the words of Psalm 78?

> We will not hide them from their children, but tell to the coming generation the glorious deeds of the Lord, and his might, and the wonders which he has wrought. He established a testimony in Jacob, and appointed a law in Israel, which he commanded our fathers to teach to their children; that the next generation might know them, the children yet unborn, and arise and tell them to their children, so that they should set their hope in God, and not forget the works of God, but keep his commandments (Ps 78:4-7).

It is not only the depth of this concern that challenges us. It is also the effectiveness of the communication. As we have seen, the emphasis fell on provoking response as much as on simple telling. Moreover the faith was communicated across the generation gap not just by specialized religious instruction, but in the normal patterns of everyday living.

> And these words which I command you this day shall be upon your heart; and you shall teach them diligently to your children, and shall talk of them when you sit in your house, and when you walk by the way, and when you lie down, and when you rise (Deut 6:6-7).

Life-to-life

The Israelites were not communicating just theological propositions; they were communicating life. The only proper medium for such communication was life itself. The faith had to be lived out. Just speaking about it was not enough. It had to be immediately relevant to everyday living, and it had to be seen to be relevant.

The biblical faith has always been meant to be communicated as a 'culture', a total way of life, in the context of personal relationships and shared experiences. Faith is to be experienced as a life-commitment by adults who act as models to the young. It has to be communicated in both concrete and abstract form, through adult modelling and through verbal communication.

The younger generation had to experience the truth of the faith in the lives of the older generation, as well as listening to the propositions of the faith on the lips of the older generation. The Israelites were to teach their young as they sat at home and as they walked by the way, as they lay down and when they got up. An adult's testimony to a conversion experience years ago is not as helpful for a young person as that adult's present experience of relating the faith to the problems of life here and now.

So we have not stumbled upon some quaint characteristics of Israelite family life when we study the wearing of phylacteries or the writing of texts from the Torah on the doorway. These practices sprang from the two verses which follow the passage in Deuteronomy 6. The Israelites were to teach God's commands diligently to their children in everyday life—'And you shall bind them as a sign upon your hand, and they shall be as frontlets between your eyes. And you shall write them on the doorposts of your house and on your gates' (Deut 6:8-9). Like circumcision and animal sacrifice, they show the same compulsion to communicate clearly to the young the fact that the Lord is a God relevant to every aspect of every human being's life. So life itself has to be the medium for that communication.

There is a principle here which has a wider application than religious instruction within the family. Jesus instructed his disciples by living alongside them and inviting them to share his life as well as listen to his words. When he first called the twelve, he appointed them primarily 'to be with him' (Mk 3:14).

It is clear that they understood the importance of this life-to-life discipling because, when they chose a successor for Judas Iscariot, Peter stated the criterion on which he should be selected:

> So one of the men who have accompanied us during all the time that the Lord Jesus went in and out among us, beginning from the baptism of John until the day when he was taken up from us—one of these men must become with us a witness to his resurrection (Acts 1:21-22).

It was a long-term exposure to the life of Jesus that determined the choice of Matthias to take the place of Judas.

The ministry of Jesus, however, raises a particularly interesting question: was he evangelizing or was he discipling the twelve disciples?

It is not a distinction we can easily make. Clearly the process was a continuous one and the method was consistent—he lived alongside them and opened his life to them. The medium of communication was not just the spoken word; it was the lived life which, although it included a great many spoken words, was not restricted to them.

Neither evangelism (the communication of the faith to the outsider) nor discipling (the building up in the faith of the convert) will be effective unless they apply this clear biblical principle. The search for effective programmes will fail. In God's service there are only effective people.

There are some significant features of Jesus' method to note. There was an extended time involved. Jesus' instruction of the twelve was no crash course. It had begun before he formally called the twelve of them to follow him (they already belonged to a group who were following him Luke 6:13), and it continued until the crucifixion and even afterwards. It relied on an extended period of low-key communication, not on a brief period of intense communication.

There was also a high degree of commitment and intimacy involved. Even though one of the disciples was going to betray him (and that is an important fact to remember), Jesus kept nothing back from his closest circle of associates. He made a clear distinction between them and the wider circles of his followers—'He did not speak to them [the crowds] without a parable, but privately to his own disciples he explained everything' (Mk 4:34). He lived with them and gave himself to them.

Then there was a clear focus in Jesus' method. While he must have touched the lives of a great many people, he was content to make a significant impact on the lives of just a few. It is this aspect of Jesus' work that is most widely ignored in youth work today, and it is one to which I must return before long. But first there is some more to say about this whole principle of communication.

The ministry of Jesus with the apostles cannot by itself provide the normal pattern for Christian youth work. Clearly his ministry was unique. The twelve apostles are a special case. The indicatives in the gospels should not be taken as imperatives. So we cannot just argue directly from the way Jesus worked with the twelve to the way we should work with young people today.

We see, however, the same pattern emerging in the rest of the New Testament. Paul wrote to the Thessalonians: 'We were ready to share with you not only the gospel of God but also our own selves' (1 Thess 2:8). Like Jesus, Paul travelled with a small band of companions with whom he shared his life. When he found himself separated from them, he suffered great distress (see 2 Tim 4:9-22).

Paul communicated the faith life-to-life and the epistles show that this principle was well understood. 'Be imitators of me, as I am of Christ,' wrote Paul (1 Cor 11:1). It sounds bigheaded, but Paul knew perfectly well that it would happen anyway. He had to be like Christ because it was the truth of his life that the Corinthians would learn! He commended the Thessalonians because they 'became imitators of us and of the Lord' and in turn 'became an example to all the believers in Macedonia and in Achaia' (1 Thess 1:5-7). The writer to the Hebrews told his readers that they should imitate the faith of their leaders (Heb 13:7). Peter told church leaders that they must set an example to their flock (1 Pet 5:3).

A clear-cut distinction between evangelizing and discipling cannot be made in the epistles either. The gospel 'came' to the Colossians when they 'learned it from Epaphras' (Col 1:5-7). The gospel is not just proclaimed or preached. It is also learnt and taught. For the Ephesians to 'learn Christ' was for them both to 'hear about him' and to be 'taught in him' (Eph 4:20-21).

In the West we are accustomed to think of the 'truth' as a disembodied abstract. The Bible does not see it in this way. When Pilate asked his famous question, 'What is truth?' Jesus had already provided his disciples with the answer: 'I am the way, the truth, and the life.' The biblical measure of truth is the person of Jesus Christ. Truth in the Bible is a quality of persons, primarily, and of propositions only secondarily.[36] So the communication of that truth is from one whole person to another whole person. It is less than the whole truth if it involves less than the whole person.

The passionate concern to pass the faith to the next generation that runs through the Bible was linked to a concern to find the most powerful ways to do it, and to commit the whole of life to the task. These are important principles for youth ministry. Does the work of our own churches match up to these biblical principles, or does it owe more to the 'classroom' model of Western education? Perhaps the very term 'Sunday School' gives the game away. We need to get back to the Bible and to look at what it is teaching us with fresh eyes. Even the insights of modern educational psychology are less valuable for building an effective bridge across the generation gap than the insights of the Old Testament. There we discover that we must encourage questioning, we must stress direct experience, we must build on the lived moment, and we must ensure that faith is experienced as a life-commitment by living models.

The basic method of evangelism

What precise conclusions can we draw for youth evangelism from this principle of communication that the Bible is so insistent about? How do our normal approaches to evangelism match up to it?

The foundation of evangelism is a long-term, personal, deep commitment of an individual Christian to an individual non-Christian. Just as Jesus called his disciples individually and committed himself to them individually, so there is no short cut available to us whereby we can start to reach lots of people quickly. We can't and we won't.

The Acts of the Apostles and the history of Christianity do record occasions when large numbers have responded at one time to the gospel, but these do not seem to be the norm. The story of Paul's missionary journeys is not a story of spectacular numbers responding with alacrity to his message. More often a handful accepted, the majority were indifferent, and a significant number were provoked to intense opposition.

When he wrote the second letter to Timothy, probably his final epistle, Paul clearly looked back on his ministry with mixed feelings: 'You are aware that all who are in Asia turned away from me,' he wrote (2 Tim 1:15). It must have been particularly bitter since Luke records that a few years before, during Paul's two and a half years' stay in Ephesus, 'all the residents of Asia heard the word of the Lord' and many believed (Acts 19:1, 2, 10). Now 'all in Asia' had turned away from him. A great awakening had been followed by a great defection. 'To every eye but that of faith,' H.C.G. Moule commented on this passage, 'it must have appeared just then as if the gospel were on the eve of extinction.'[37] We like to skim over such passages, but we must be cautious of the tendency to view the growth of the New Testament church through rose-tinted spectacles.

On the surface of history there have been great successes and great reverses. But over the centuries, the community of believers has grown steadily and invisibly throughout the world. That is God's work. Our commitment is not to success, but to do what God commands us to do faithfully. In his Son he has given us a clear pattern to follow.

So youth evangelism does not consist of spraying the gospel over an open youth club, or inserting an awkward and incongruous 'God slot' into the middle of it, or hoping that the presence of one or two Christian workers will somehow infect a large group of non-Christian young people with whom they are in contact. I am not saying that these are not worthwhile activities and that God will not bless them, and sometimes use them to convert young people. He does. But they do not match the model he has himself provided for us.

Much Christian energy has been spent on models of evangelism that derive ultimately from secular rather than biblical thinking, and many Christian tears have been shed over the poverty of the results. Christians need to listen to what sociologists and psychologists and political thinkers can teach us about reaching unchurched people groups in our society. But God has already shown us the way he would have us reach them. It was the way he went himself when he became flesh and dwelt among us.

This was not a strategy or a structure or a programme. It was a personal, individual commitment. Although what Jesus achieved on the cross was universal and eternal in its significance, in becoming a man he actually restricted his direct influence to a few people in one particular place at one particular time. But from that limited, historical incarnation have sprung the redeemed people of God, as the message of salvation has been passed from one individual to another individual right down to today. With the presence of Jesus' Spirit in each of his followers, his influence today is wider than it has ever been.

As God became a man to communicate with men, so the most effective communication is from equal to equal. Many adult Christian youth workers see themselves as youth evangelists. God certainly gives special gifts of youth evangelism to certain people, but the most effective communicators of the gospel to young people will always be other young people. Discussing the issue of adolescent rebellion against adult authority figures (parents, teachers, etc.) Tom Kitwood writes:

> . . . many boys and girls, especially during the early teenage years, simply exchange one type of authority for another. Those of approximately the same age often appear better guides, because they are more able to show what is appropriate not only in a symbolic, but also in a concrete way.[38]

We should note that last sentence. Young people need to discover faith in a concrete way, and the most concrete way is in the life of another young person whom they get to know well. Adult models of faith are important, but the most immediate impact will be the faith of another young person or, better still, the faith of a group of young people. There is an obvious difficulty for the adult Christian youth worker, trying to control a lively open youth club and so inevitably being an authority figure for its members, who is also seeking to be the primary evangelist of those young people.

What I am saying here, both about communication and about evangelism, is well illustrated by a common feature of much Christian youth work: frequently the leaders of Christian youth fellowships are disappointed when they arrange an outreach event and ask the Christian young people to bring their non-Christian friends to it. The number of non-Christians who turn up on the night is very few. The young Christians understand the message that they are meant to bring their friends. They agree with it. But they find it very hard to do in practice.

One reason is that the young people do not see the youth leaders bringing their own adult non-Christian friends to adult outreach events. We think that we can teach evangelism without modelling evangelism. We are asking our young people to invite their peers, so they must see us inviting our peers.

Many youth workers make the mistake of thinking that, because they are involved in youth work, it is their entire evangelistic work for Christ. How many of us have given up trying to win our friends and neighbours for Christ because we are concentrating on our Christian work with the youth club? It is easier for me to chat about Jesus to a teenager in the youth group than to raise the same subject with the working man who lives next door to me.

Church fellowships can make the same mistake. When faced with the problem of their lack of impact on a particular part of their catchment area (perhaps a deprived council estate), they come up with the solution of opening a youth club there. While that is in itself an excellent thing, it is not an acceptable evangelistic strategy to solve the problem. The Bible supplies us with surprisingly little warrant for evangelizing other people's children. The adults in the church have a responsibility to reach out to the adults on the estate. They should not be allowed to evade that responsibility by passing the evangelistic buck to a couple of their workers who are given a mandate to take the gospel to the teenagers on the estate by opening a youth club.

Evangelism is not some special activity that adults do to young people (or—worse still—that 'missionaries' do to 'natives'). It is the natural—and inevitable—fruit of a healthy Christian life. It will be part of all our contacts with other people. Once it ceases to be that and starts to be a special activity that we confine to our youth work, we are not only inhibiting our own spiritual lives, we are also disabling our youth work because we cannot teach what we are not doing ourselves.

A main qualification for Christian youth work should be an individual's ability to share the gospel with his or her own equals. It seems extraordinary that we commission people for all forms of missionary service without first making sure that they have shown themselves capable of bringing one of their own friends to Christ. The deep, individual, long-term, personal commitment that this demands should be the foundational requirement for full-time Christian service. So much of the Christian church is weak in its impact on society because we have allowed evangelism to become a specialist, results-orientated activity, and not the calling of every Christian to commit his or her life, in depth, over many years, to one or two others, in order to win just them to Jesus Christ.

We think that we can equip people to communicate the gospel across barriers of age, race, class and culture, when they have not yet communicated Jesus to even one of their own close friends. We think that we can change the structure of our society and the social injustices of our world, when we are not actually managing to convert the individuals who make up that society. We need to regain this vision that the task of winning our world for God is a low-profile, unsensational, long-term task involving you and me. *We* are the primary evangelists—the Billy Grahams and Luis Palaus are not. God has equipped them with tremendous gifts of communication and evangelism in order to give them to us as evangelistic tools for *our* ministry.

It is this model of evangelism that will show us the way to cross the barriers that divide our society and our world. It is the one-to-one commitment of the individual Christian to the non-Christian that provides a bridge that can span the gap created by social, cultural, educational and ethnic differences. I find it very hard to relate to a group of people from an entirely different background to myself, but faced with one or two individuals the task becomes manageable. In fact, I find that after a time I am less and less aware that there is even a problem, as the individuals become more and more important to me and I am more and more familiar to them.

Working with West Indian and mixed-race teenagers in Balham, it is not the large cultural differences between our various backgrounds that we see. We see one another: Mark, Jimmy, Kelvin, JB, Simon, Demetrious, Marc, Martin. We meet as friend to friend, establishing and building relationships over the five years we have known each other. When Jimmy (with a mum from Guyana and a dad from Nigeria) sits down regularly with me (the son of a retired British army colonel) and we study the Bible together, the gap between our contrasting backgrounds fades into insignificance.

This gap will not be spanned by policies and strategies and church committees. It can only be crossed by individuals opening their lives to individuals. We need to be cautious about projects and initiatives that analyse statistics and make recommendations about the evangelization of our society. We need to beware particularly of those telling the church about evangelism who are not themselves evangelizing.

This is particularly a lesson for the youth worker. How can we communicate about evangelism? By doing it ourselves. Our evangelistic zeal must express itself in the commitment of our lives to one or two people of our own age, as well as to the young people we work with. We must ourselves be an example of what we are trying to teach. Otherwise the next generation will be as bad at telling other people about Jesus as so many of us are.

Concrete communication

At this point we must turn our attention once again from evangelism to the wider issue of communication. The way Jesus communicated with his disciples has been helpfully described in four stages:
1. I tell: you listen.
2. I do: you watch.
3. You do: I watch.
4. You do and report back to me.
It begins with telling. We start with a message in words. There is no other place to start. If we try to start at another point, our communication will be confused. We worship and proclaim a God who speaks and who has spoken in history. Woe

betide us if we are not faithful to his words![39]

All too often, however, the communication of the Christian faith confines itself to the spoken word: we told them and they listened. They listened so nicely that, having finished telling them, we told them some more; and, as they listened very nicely to that too, we told them even more afterwards. No wonder they find it hard to do! They have never seen it done.

We cannot communicate the Christian faith as though it were an academic subject at school. It is not that we do not need to learn it as thoroughly as we learn Mathematics or History. We need to learn it much more thoroughly. We need all the insights that modern education can bring us. But they will not be adequate for the task.

> . . . the assumption that it is possible by the simple process of telling to pass on knowledge in useful form . . . is the great delusion of the ages. If the learning process is to be effective, something dynamic must take place in the learner (Charles I. Gragg *Because Wisdom Can't Be Told*).

Christianity will stretch our minds and it will require mental effort from us. We devalue the God we worship when we give him less intellectual energy than we give to subjects at school or college, or career exams. But the Christian faith must also challenge the will. It must make its impact on the emotions. It must be related to attitudes and abilities. It must lead to decision and to obedience.

In the Western World we have moved away from the Hebrew idea of learning which Jesus had, and have adopted a Greek view which separates what goes on in the mind from what goes on in the body and its surroundings. Our educational system makes us think in terms of the classroom as the location for learning, and the lesson or lecture as the method of presentation. We have moved a long way from the 'experimental' methods Jesus used. 'We have mistaken intellectual beliefs for faith, and teaching (the school-instruction model) for education' (John Westerhoff).

Sometimes it is those who are most committed to the faithful presentation of the message which Jesus taught, who are least aware that their style of teaching is utterly different from his. (Perhaps this may explain the gap we are often aware of, in our own and other Christians' lives, between what we say we believe and the way we live out that belief.)

A study of the way Jesus taught the disciples in Luke chapters 5 to 9 provides the model for our own work with young people today. There we see the primacy of teaching. The spoken word, whether to the crowds or to an individual, provides the basis for learning experiences. These experiences involve Jesus' actions and the disciples' actions (Lk 9:1-6).

It is actually stage three of the four stages that is least evident in the gospels' record of Jesus' practice, but stage four is quite clear (Lk 9:10). If we read on into the Acts of the Apostles, we discover stage five: 'You tell: someone else listens,' and stage six: 'You do: someone else watches,' and so it has gone on down the ages until we ourselves came to believe and to be taught the faith.

Our method of communicating the faith must be built on this biblical pattern rather than on a classroom model. The faith is not to be taught like a foreign language at school. It is to be taught in the way a child learns his own language during the ordinary processes of living. Only in this way can the all-encompassing scope of the faith be grasped. It is seen to relate to everything in life.

Most of us know our own language very much better than we know a language which we learned at school, but the process of learning was not particularly irksome or painful. I remember struggling with *être* and *connaître* at school, but I never remember as a child saying to someone who corrected my English, 'Not another one of those wretched irregular verbs!' Most of the time I was not even aware I was learning the language.

We are communicating a way of life. In his excellent book *Youth Ministry,* Lawrence Richards writes this: 'The youth leader is not primarily a talker or organiser. He is a model, a person who by the power of his own Christian example motivates dedication to Jesus Christ.'[40]

So when I lead a youth group Bible study in my front room on how a Christian should not be conformed to this world, a single glance at their surroundings will be enough to confirm or destroy the lessons of Romans 12:2 ('Do not be conformed to this world, but be transformed by the renewal of your mind . . .'). The decor of my living room is a powerful and concrete message about how a Christian is (or is not) conformed to this world. The next week we might be looking at Romans 13 and a Christian's obedience to authority, but the drive home in the passenger seat of my car afterwards will again authenticate or destroy in concrete terms the message of the Bible study. Did my driving show real respect for authority?

If this is the way that the faith must be communicated, what does it mean for youth work?

6

The Telling of Wisdom

Evangelizing and discipling young people (ii)

If the communication of the Christian faith, both to the believing and to the non-believing young person, is such a total process involving the whole life of the communicator, then there are four important consequences:

1. The limitations of print

It will make us aware of the limitations of the printed word as a medium for communication. John Benington has written, 'The extent of the modern young person's aversion to the printed word and his preference for the more direct, visual and sensory channels of communication have still not been sufficiently realised.' He continued:

> Music and dancing are among the two most important channels of 'sub-verbal communication' among young people. They are particularly appropriate means of expression as they communicate direct feeling more than precise meaning, and thus satisfy the teenager's preference for a 'life of sensation rather than thought'.[41]

The 'electric technology'—television, radio, telephone, film, video, computers—envelops us in a total barrage of sound, light and image, with which the young are now more at home than they are with the printed page.

We still have a verbal message to communicate—we cannot escape that—but there are strict limits to the effectiveness of the printed page to communicate it. In the West we have stressed the need for the Christian to have a 'quiet time', a time of personal Bible reading and prayer, and it has proved a valuable and beneficial discipline, but for fifteen centuries the Christian faith spread through the world before the invention of the printing press made personal Bible reading a possibility for large numbers of Christians.

It *is* possible to be a Christian without being able to read. We must not develop patterns of spirituality which deny that. But, having become a Christian, it is likely that a young person will want to develop and improve reading skills in order to satisfy the hunger for God's word which the Spirit has put into his heart.

It is certainly important to prevent one implied message behind a youth group programme: that God really prefers those who can read the Bible aloud fluently. We must de-emphasize academic ability as a value within the group. Too many of our young people are being made to feel below average, if not actually dumb, by their school experience. It is vital for them to learn that God does not view them in that way.

The message about God's love for man comes in words, revealed in the Bible, but we have to express it in such a way that even those who prefer a 'life of sensation rather than thought' can begin to think about it, to grapple with it, and to respond to it. In an unofficial survey conducted by Gavin Reid during three years of his ministry prior to Mission England, he found that 73.5% of all conversions were accounted for by the most 'natural' factors—the activities and life of the local church (27.8%), a Christian family background (25.8%), and Christian friends (19.9%). Specific evangelistic projects accounted for 13.2%, but Christian literature for only 2.3%. He commented:

> The importance of the person-to-person element comes through strongly in the survey and the impersonal medium of print is seen to be far less significant . . . my guess is that there are clear limits to the evangelistic effectiveness of the medium and it needs to be seen as a handmaid to more personal forms of ministry. . . . The overall impression gained here is that people become Christians through other people. . . . If our evangelism hasn't strong personal and community factors, it is hardly likely to be effective.[42]

There is a place for Christian literature and I will return later to the urgent need to root the Christian faith in the minds and the understandings of young people. Nevertheless, we must look for more powerful means of communication as the mainstay of our discipling and our evangelism.

2. Priority to contact situations

We need to look for every opportunity for the young non-Christian to live his or her life alongside the Christian, and for the new Christian to live alongside the older Christian. It is not more meetings that are needed, but more informal opportunities for the faith to flow from one life to another. We live hectic, pressurized, individual lives, but God calls us out of our individual isolation into a community of faith where he can be silently and invisibly at work between one life and another. So we will have to find ways to open up our lives to the young people we are working with. Two hours after church on a Sunday night with a dozen teenagers and an hour's preparation at another point in the week is not adequate youth ministry.

Jesus spent most of his time with his disciples, whether it was leisure time, routine living, or work. Jesus made plans for his disciples. He monitored their development and had visions for their future ministry. He spent hours in prayer for them. He challenged them. He gave them jobs to do, pushing them out into more activity and responsibility, giving them the freedom to fail. When he was doing things, he took his disciples with him, so that they could learn by watching him in action. He allowed them to see him weak and troubled. (In fact, he seemed particularly concerned that they should witness one of his greatest moments of suffering when he woke the three disciples in Gethsemane. See Matthew 26:36-46.) He continued even to attend to them as he was dying on the cross.

We know that there was a uniqueness about the ministry of Jesus, but all too often we are concerned that our young people should see only our strengths. We want a 'pedestal' ministry, where they look up to us as great youth leaders: strong, in control, unflappable, witty, attractive, intelligent, popular, up-market, with street credibility and generally 'neat'! We want our youth programmes to run without a hitch, so that word gets round that this is the youth group to come to—everyone has fun, everyone laughs, it's brilliant, fast-moving, up-tempo, exciting.

Jesus, however, ensured that his disciples saw him weak and in pain. We forget that God's power is often revealed in weakness. When our young people see us weak and fallible, making fools of ourselves, with our brittle dignity shattered, they may feel closer to us and love us more than at any previous time in the relationship. We must learn to abandon our dignity and our fear of failure. It is when they see us fail and suffer that the model we are providing for them becomes real. They need to see us demonstrate appropriate ways to express anger and pain and grief, as the disciples saw Jesus do.

We should certainly try to run excellent youth programmes, but we must also allow young people far enough into our lives to see us as we really are. There is a great need for honesty. Young people need honest answers to their questions. They need to find integrity in the lives of Christian adults. It is easy for a degree of hypocrisy to appear in the life of the youth leader. One Christian speaker,with an international ministry, told me that for twenty years no one had asked him whether he was reading his Bible and praying.

So priority must be given to developing contact situations. We must maximize the opportunity to do things together. Most of us cannot fit many more engagements into our week, so we need to look at the life we are already living for opportunities to share it with others. I am always amazed at the interest teenagers show in the lives of adults—their eagerness to spend time in a youth leader's home; their willingness to help with apparently routine and humdrum tasks, like gardening or redecorating; the speed with which they volunteer for any task so long as it is clearly a part of the adult world and not a part of the world of childhood.

At the start of Greenbelt one year I asked a West Indian friend whether he would like to come and help me mow the lawn of the cottage where I was staying. As soon as I had asked the question, I thought what an idiot I was. Here was the foremost Christian pop festival with a hundred and one bright and brilliant entertainments for the young, and I had asked this young man to come and mow a lawn. I tried to backtrack and withdraw the request, but he was not taking no for an answer. He was determined to come and mow that lawn. It seemed to him an adult thing to do and therefore preferable to the world of Christian teenage entertainment. Such is the aspiration of the young to share in the adult world.

For some of us it may even be possible to share parts of our working lives with the young. It may be worth having 'any driver' insurance cover for our car, so that when we have to take a trip we can ask an older member of the youth fellowship to come as a driver or companion on the journey. What better opportunity for discipling in responsible and courteous driving, and in the use of other people's possessions? (The thought of other people driving our cars is also an interesting challenge to the insidious grip our possessions have over us!)

A young family provides another valuable focus for teenage attention. This is not just a matter of baby-sitting, but of allowing our children to grow up in an extended family where they are cared for and form deep relationships with other young people. Teenagers with personality problems are sometimes relaxed and put at ease by the company of small children.

The youth leader's marriage and family life must not be put at risk by his youth ministry (I will say more about the family, both of the young person and the youth worker, in chapter eight), but young people will benefit from seeing the youth leader in his family—praying with his children, asking their forgiveness, making mistakes and apologizing to his wife. We do not have to be perfect (or even good) before God can use us as a model.

It is important to discover ways to integrate youth ministry into the whole of our adult lives—not struggling to squeeze in yet another evening when we can invite the gang round to our flat for coffee—but looking for the things we are already doing that we can start doing *with* them. Most of the time in those chapters in Luke (5-9) the disciples were simply 'with' Jesus. He carried on with his ministry of teaching and healing the crowds, but all the time he had an eye on the twelve. It may be right for a youth leader to give up certain things in order to give more time and attention to youth leadership (God means many of us to do rather less, but to do it better). But one dimension of youth leadership is inviting young people to join us in our world, not trying to find the time to ape their lifestyle in their world.

The key to effective Christian youth work is people— people in whose lives Christ is alive, and who will open themselves to young people, not to talk down to them, nor to dominate them with attractive and charismatic personalities, but to show them how to love one another as Christ commanded us. 'Personal work' is fundamental to youth work. We have to build personal relationships. We have to maximize opportunities for life-to-life discipling, where we can live alongside young people and they can absorb the Christian faith from the atmosphere around them.

That is why houseparties, camps and weekends away with the youth club provide such a powerful opportunity in Christian youth work. It may be that the normal pattern of our programme is too dull, too cerebral, too culturally conditioned and too unbiblical in its methods, and time spent away camping, youth hostelling or on a Christian holiday provides a more total spiritual experience. For example, the female youth leader, whom a girl hears explaining the doctrine of the cross at a morning meeting, may have a game of tennis with her before lunch, talk to her about her parents' divorce over lunch, walk down the shops with her in the afternoon, study the Bible and pray with her in the evening, and sleep in the next bed, or the next room, at night. There is a real exposure of life to life. In a weekend's camping most of our pretences have been stripped away by the second morning, particularly if it is raining.

These activities also have enormous potential for the training of leaders. As a new leader works alongside a more experienced leader in such a total form of ministry for twenty-four hours a day, the learning process is greatly accelerated. In a little-noticed paragraph in his autobiography, David Watson provided an extraordinary testimony to what he learnt for his future ministry from residential youth activities:

Undoubtedly the most formative influence of my faith during the five years at Cambridge was my involvement with the boys' houseparties, or 'Bash camps' as they were generally known. Over the five years I went to no less than thirty-five of these camps: two at Christmas, two at Easter and three in the summer of each year. They were tremendous opportunities for learning the very basics of Christian ministry. Through patient and detailed discipling (although that word was never used) I learned, until it became second nature, how to lead a person to Christ, how to answer common questions, how to follow up a young convert, how to lead a group Bible study, how to give a Bible study to others, how to prepare and give a talk, how to pray, how to teach others to pray, how to write encouraging letters, how to know God's guidance, how to overcome temptation, and also, most important, how to laugh and have fun as a Christian—how not to become too intense, if you like. I also gained excellent grounding in basic Christian doctrines, with strong emphasis being placed on clarity and simplicity. All this was being constantly modelled by those who were much more mature in the faith, and I may never fully realise how much I owe to the amazing, detailed, personal help that I received over those five years. No Christian organization is perfect, of course; and it would be easy to find fault with a group as powerful and effective as this one. But if God has given me a useful ministry in any area today, the roots of it were almost certainly planted during those remarkable five years in the camps. It was the best possible training I could have received.[43]

Getting away from home is another important factor. It represents a step towards adulthood, and it also provides a distancing from the familiar, which allows a greater freedom of thought about attitudes and values. It also causes certain problems because residential Christian activities are by their very nature exceptional. They are not a normal experience of the Christian life. There may be problems in relating the more intense spiritual experiences of a camp or houseparty to the more ordinary spiritual life back at home. Leaders need to give careful thought to this. It may be wise to play down the emotional intensity of a Christian houseparty or camp so that it does not contrast too sharply with the life of the youth fellowship at home. The sad spiritual sag in the life of the teenager that can follow a time away from home is a familiar phenomenon, but wise leadership can minimize its long-term effect.

Young people have a need for adventure in order to change, discover and grow. While physical adventure can meet this need, 'adventure' is not confined to physical activities. The adventure of meeting new people and handling new social situations is even more valuable in a young person's development.

As the teenage years go by, the young person gets less interested in *what* they are going to do and more interested in *whom* they are going to be doing it with. The first question a teenager tends to ask when invited to a function is: 'Who is going?' Girls mature faster than boys in this respect, and boys remain activity-orientated longer, but older teenagers are usually less interested in the activity programme of a camp or houseparty and more interested in its social aspects.

Planning for youth ministry should show a priority to contact situations, because there the communication of faith will be at its strongest. There is a great value in going away together (whether on a do-it-yourself weekend, or on a nationally-run Christian camp or houseparty). Youth leaders who have not tried this do not know what they are missing. Youth leaders who have will not need me to say any more.

3. The value of the peer group

If the faith is communicated so effectively through life contact, then the influence young people exercise upon one another will be enormous. I have already commented on the difficulty someone under sixteen experiences in holding a set of values different from that of his or her friends and contemporaries. I noted our need to provide a community of faith as part of our evangelism, so that the young person has immediate and concrete examples of believing to copy.[44]

The Christian life is about change: the transformation of the individual into the image of Christ and the change this then produces in his social environment. But change is a community process.

Counselling can never be the heart of an effective ministry. Growth toward maturity, and the healing that often must take place in persons before they are free to grow, comes essentially though involvement with others in the process of ministry—particularly through Body relationships and Scripture. The church of the New Testament is a transforming *community*, and transformation is a community transaction, not primarily a transaction between two persons . . .[45]

Change is often painful and frightening. The Christian peer group has to provide a new environment in which change becomes possible for the young person. He is not asked to change alone. He is asked to change together with others. He has examples to copy, and in time he himself becomes an example to others. It involves a process of social interaction. Without this we cannot expect young people to live distinctive Christian lives in a world that is so strongly opposed to Christ. They are called to make a heroic stand against the values of that world, but God provides them with brothers and sisters in Christ to support and encourage them in this revolution.

Christian camps and houseparties provide an example of how good teenagers can be at communicating faith to one another. One youth group can have a tremendous ministry to another when they meet up on a residential event. Indeed, spiritual growth in a group, although less spectacular, is often more significant in the long run than spiritual growth in an individual. God deals with each of us as individuals, but he calls us to a communal life as Christians, dependent on one another from the beginning to the end. The normal New Testament word for the Christian is 'saint'. Of sixty-two occurrences, sixty-one are in the plural, and even then the only exception is Philippians 4:21—'Greet every saint'! We grow in the Christian life together.

Where isolated individual growth occurs it can be vulnerable. When a young person goes away by herself on a Christian activity without a friend or a leader from her home fellowship, the experience may be very exciting, but it is also abnormal. She is not normally away from home, on holiday, in mainly young company, and in a Christian environment where there are powerful experiences of communal worship and convincing explanations of Christianity. The more abnormal the experience, the less lasting its effect may be. If she has a sense of returning from space travel when she gets home at the end, it is not easy for her to believe that she is still in the same world. Powerful new resolutions may be made, but a week or ten days is not a long time to work them out. There can follow an equally powerful reaction, devastating in its effect on the spiritual life of the young person.

The same experience shared by a group of young people who meet together regularly through the rest of the year will be less intoxicating. It will not seem so strange and so exciting, and it will probably be longer lasting in its effect on their spiritual lives. What happened on the Christian camp or houseparty becomes part, not just of the individual's life, but of the group's life. Such progress was a real part of the development of the whole group. It was probably less sensational because of the continuity with home (there could be less pretence), but it was also more permanent. So opportunities to take young people away together should not be missed.

We are ministering to groups as well as to individuals. It may be possible to set up small support groups of four or five young people within a larger fellowship. These groups are committed to one another in depth—particularly to support and motivate each other for evangelism. If they are to be effective, there must be a serious resolve not to disengage from one another for a given period. Some groups even use the idea of a 'contract' that they enter into with one another for a certain number of months.[46]

At this level there can be a much deeper sharing of personal problems and joys. One leader working in depth with four or five young people who meet together regularly, in addition to a larger, weekly, fellowship meeting, is a pattern that has proved very useful in Christian youth work.

The problem of cliques

There is a frequent misunderstanding among youth leaders

about the relationship between fellowship and evangelism: 'They are just an inward-looking clique. They are too committed to one another and they will not look outside themselves at all. They don't want any outsiders to come in and disturb their cosy, comfortable, little fellowship. I don't know how to get them involved in outreach.' So goes the complaint from the frustrated youth leader.

But I doubt it is possible for any Christian group to be *too* committed to one another. Where there are cliques, it is usually a case of an insecure group, with a good deal of concealed jealousy, rivalry and sexual competition. The girls are overaware of who is going out with whom, and the relationships are exclusive and competitive. The boys are vying with one another for the greatest share of the limelight. The group has turned in on itself and is unable to reach out to others, because of a lack of trust between its members.

Where a group of Christian young people really commit themselves to one another in love, they will start to care for one another and to share in a supernatural way. They will weep together when the parents of one of their number start divorce proceedings, and rejoice together when another gets a place at college or a job. That sort of group is characterized by a lack of sexual competitiveness and jealousy. It is able to welcome the outsider because it is secure in its internal relationships.

'By this all men will know that you are my disciples,' said Jesus, 'if you have love for one another' (Jn 13:35). Not love for the world, note, but love for one another. It is our love for one another that is one of our greatest evangelistic weapons. When a young person encounters a group of his or her contemporaries with an open, welcoming and supportive attitude, it contrasts sharply with other groups at school or in the neighbourhood.

The test is whether the group contains the sort of socially inept person who is expelled by those other groups (because they will not tolerate the odd, the strange, the difficult and the unpopular as members). Christian groups must not only accept such social outcasts; they must love and care for them. When a non-Christian sees this happen, he is convicted that he has encountered the supernatural, because he knows all too well what sort of treatment such people receive from everyone else.

Evangelism is usually a gradual attraction into a community of faith. In youth work the main evangelists will be the young people themselves. The major task for the youth leader will be to equip and enable a group of Christian young people naturally to attract others to themselves. The quality of the relationships within the group will be vital to this—we may need to teach them to become far more deeply committed to one another. All too often we cast ourselves in the role of the evangelist, and we impose our own evangelistic strategy on our young people.

There is much talk about involvement and participation in youth work. But what are we asking young people to get involved in? Is it in planning and servicing the programme, or is it in ministry to people? Too often we try to involve young people in all the wrong aspects of our youth work: planning programmes, setting up meetings, sitting on committees, and a whole range of administrative chores.

The focus of their involvement ought to be primarily on people—discipling and evangelizing. We may sometimes need to take back from them certain responsibilities which should not have been delegated in the first place (like planning the programme perhaps) and start leading them into a people-orientated ministry where they have a communication function, and not a programme- or meeting-orientated ministry where they have an organizational function. We should make them responsible for people, rather than for programmes.

It is not wrong for them to participate in the organizational aspects of youth work, like sitting on committees and taking decisions, but it is wrong for them to get the impression that this is what Christian ministry consists of. Christian ministry is about people. We want to teach them people skills—how to lead their friends to Christ, how to care for each other spiritually, how to become servant leaders in laying down their lives for one another. It is the adult leaders' task to do the more mundane work of servicing the organization, so that the young people can concentrate on the real work of ministry and leadership.

Sometimes the failure of our youth evangelism is related to the inadequacy of our nurture programme. We are not setting an example ourselves of how to reach people of our own age with the gospel. We are not equipping the young people themselves to attract outsiders into their community of faith. When we do encourage them to get involved in the work of the youth fellowship, we invite them to help us with the programme, but not with the people.

We must first teach them by example how, having committed their lives to Christ, they can commit their lives to his body here on earth; that is to a few other Christians with whom they learn to share and for whom they learn to care. Having committed their lives to Christ's body, then we must teach them (by example again) to commit their lives to his work: that is to one or two non-Christians with whom they determine to share their lives and the gospel. Commitment to Christ, commitment to his body, commitment to his work— that is a helpful threefold aim for our ministry with young people. We are not training them to chair committees, plan programmes or organize meetings; we are training them to convert and transform the world.

4. Focus of ministry

If faith is to be communicated in the total, life-to-life manner that Jesus used, then we will have to limit our sphere of influence as tightly as he limited his. It is striking how narrowly Jesus focused his ministry.

For a Jew living in the first century A.D., the whole world

was divided sharply into two groups: the Jews and the Gentiles. Jesus concentrated his ministry on the lost sheep of the house of Israel. When he encountered Gentiles, he made his priorities clear, even to the point of apparent rudeness in the case of the Syro-Phoenician woman ('. . . it is not right to take the children's bread and throw it to the dogs' Mk 7:24-30).

He did not conduct his ministry in the main centres of population where he would have drawn the greatest crowds. He appears to have moved through the countryside and villages, so that the crowds had to come out to him, sometimes to places so remote that he was concerned that the crowds would starve before they could get back to civilization (Mt 15:32).

When they came, he told them awkward and puzzling stories, which we call 'parables'. When they heard the parable of the sower (Mk 4:1-9), some no doubt shrugged their shoulders and went to look for something to eat, but others gathered round and asked what on earth he meant. 'To you,' Jesus said, 'has been given the secret of the kingdom of God, but for those outside everything is in parables' (Mk 4:11). There was a constant sieving process in Jesus' ministry. He sieved out the genuinely interested from the idly curious. He sieved out the earnest seeker from the crowds who just wanted miracles and wonders (Jn 6:26).

In John 8, Jesus was speaking to Jews in the Temple. Halfway through the chapter many started to believe in him (v. 30). So Jesus addressed himself specifically to them (v. 31). But in the verses that follow he appears to alienate them *deliberately,* until in verse 59 'they took up stones to throw at him, but Jesus hid himself, and went out of the Temple'. Such a passage shakes our preconceptions about Jesus Christ. It reveals his determination to sort out the true believer from the time-server.

At the end of John 6 this process led to an almost total desertion:

After this many of his disciples drew back and no longer went about with him. Jesus said to the twelve, 'Will you also go away?' Simon Peter answered him, 'Lord, to whom shall we go? You have the words of eternal life' (vv. 66-68).

However, even among those whose discipleship was genuine, Jesus sifted out those with whom he worked in depth. From among the crowds he picked seventy to send out in pairs (Lk 10:1), but he had a prior commitment to the twelve. Within the twelve, he picked the three, Peter, James and John. Even within those three he seems to have singled out Peter for special attention, and also perhaps 'the disciple whom Jesus loved'. We could almost say there was a deliberate 'favouritism' in the ministry of Jesus. The pre-existent Son of God, whose power had created the universe, confined his attentions while on earth to just a few people. Undoubtedly he could have influenced more people—many more were eager to come within his orbit—but there was a clear focus to his ministry.

In youth work we neglect Jesus' example at our peril. All too often youth leaders are trying to 'bless' all the young people in their care, forgetting that ten years after they have left there will only be one or two lives that will have been deeply influenced by their ministry. This is going to happen whether we like it or not, so the youth leader needs to think in these terms. Jesus certainly did. He worked outwards from strength, building up one or two in a small inner group, and then the twelve, and, from that unlikely beginning, founding a church that has spread throughout the world.

The early years of my own ministry were transformed when I suddenly realized that I would influence deeply the lives of only a few people during my first full-time post. Up to then I was happily deluding myself that I was influencing the whole of a large church. This new realization was liberating and helpful.

Business men talk about the 'Pareto principle' (that 20% of our work will achieve 80% of our results). There is no particular spiritual wisdom in that, but it is a shrewd observation of how things are in life. We may not be able to alter the fact, but at least we can be aware of it and pray over the 20%. Jesus spent a night in prayer before calling the twelve.

Every day we spend our time and energy on a great many things that will have no significance in eternity, but there are some things which do have eternal value. We may not be able to spend a greater quantity of time on them, but we can probably increase the quality of that time. We would do well to sit down, think out and pray over that 20%.

It may involve us in a sieving process too. Just as Jesus selected those to whom he gave special attention, we will want to focus our ministry on those whom God specially lays on our heart. This is essentially a process of focus, rather than that of exclusion. Three times the risen Jesus urged Peter to feed his sheep (Jn 21:15-19). We have a duty to meet spiritual hunger among our young people. If we do not satisfy spiritual hunger, we are neglecting Jesus' clear command to us.

It may not always be easy to recognize spiritual hunger. We will need God's Spirit to guide us. A hunger for the things of God may appear in a non-Christian as a willingness to give serious attention to the claims of Christ. In the Christian, it may show itself as a readiness for greater obedience to God's will. We must detect it and find ways to meet it. Sometimes hungry sheep starve, because their shepherds are too busy entertaining goats. In youth ministry, Jesus' call to us is to feed sheep, not to entertain goats.

I have already warned of the dangers of dividing young people lightly into the 'saved' and the 'unsaved', the 'sheep' and the 'goats', but it is necessary to exercise our judgement humbly and sensitively in youth ministry. We do not believe, in the final resort, that the work is ours. It is God's work. He does it through his Spirit working in the believer, and on the unbeliever. Our task is to perceive what the Spirit is doing and to join ourselves to him. Our ministry must always be in step with the Spirit. Keeping in that relationship may be harder and more humbling than we expected, but God's Spirit is at work, and whatever he does will last for ever.

When we focus our ministries on a few people, we are trying to find out what it is that God is wanting to do through us. It is humbling to discover it is rather less than we ourselves thought we could do! But we have the example of Jesus Christ. That encourages us to realize the effectiveness of this way of working.

We long to make disciples of all nations. That is God's command to us and we are determined to take it seriously, but the question is, how can we do it?

If we want to obey Christ's command, we must follow Christ's example. That is God's way of reaching men. When a youth leader begins to focus his or her ministry, it does not mean that he or she has no concern for the others in the youth club. It is a sign of an increased concern for them, because that leader is now taking seriously Jesus' own method of reaching people. If we really love people and have a longing to reach them, then we will confine the focus of our attention to a few. Otherwise we rate ourselves above Jesus, and think that we can do what he could not.

This principle of focusing our ministry highlights the need for corporate (rather than solo) leadership. The normal New Testament pattern of leadership is corporate (Jesus sending the disciples out in twos, Paul and his travelling companions, the references to elders in Acts 20:17, Titus 1:5, James 5:14, etc). Wherever possible that should be the pattern in youth work today. Where two or more leaders work together, each can focus his or her own ministry, and by prayerful planning, an overview and strategy for the whole group of young people can be maintained as well. It is part of a leader's responsibility to oversee and care for all the group. To do this effectively, he will need to work with other leaders (unless the group is very small) and to focus his own ministry on a few.

Those few will be the ones in whose lives we detect God to be at work. They may already be clearly committed to the

Christian faith, or they may not yet be. We look for confirmation from God's Spirit that it is his purpose to use us to help
them.

It may be possible to build something into our programmes
that provides a sieve for genuine spiritual hunger. Youth
leaders have sometimes started a small prayer meeting, or
something similar, without any of the trappings that might
attract people for secondary reasons: no coffee, no comfortable surroundings, no social time. Many a leader has been
surprised at those who have turned up for such a meeting,
because it has revealed spiritual hunger in unexpected places.

Spiritual hunger can go undetected when cultural barriers
conceal it. A young person with reading difficulties is unlikely
to show much enthusiasm for the sort of Bible study that puts
a great emphasis on the ability to read. Only persistent prayer
will allow us to see young people as God sees them, and to
understand what he is doing—and what he wants to do—in
their lives. Along with prayer, there is the increased wisdom
that shared leadership brings. If we can discuss individuals
with one, or more, other leaders, it will increase the accuracy
of our assessment of those individuals. There is much more
yet to be said about youth leadership teams, but one great
gain of having other leaders alongside us is the increased
insight it provides into our ministries and into the young
people we are working with.

For the Christian youth leader, to focus ministry and to feed
sheep are not popular strategies. The leader, whose chief
desire is for a popular and outwardly successful ministry,
would do well to neglect them. Even the leader whose aim is
to be obedient to Jesus (rather than to be successful), will be
under constant pressure to meet the expressed needs of the
majority who clamour for attention. It is our faith in Jesus
Christ that assures us that the greatest need of the majority
can only be met by our obedience, not only to his command
(to make disciples of all nations), but also to the example he
set for us (to focus on a few). If we do that faithfully, then

God will multiply the results of our ministry, and through the people we help he will be able to help many others also.

The call to maturity

To work in this way requires great maturity in the youth leader. That is a very necessary quality for youth leadership, because there is a clear call to maturity throughout the Bible. No leader can impart to young people what he has not begun to acquire for himself.[47]

This call to maturity is evident in 'the invitation to wisdom' with which the Bible responds to the young person's aspiration to adulthood (and which we have already considered).[48] It is not a call 'to grow up'. It is a call to the completeness that only God can bring to a human being, whatever his age. 'Remember also your Creator in the days of your youth, before the evil days come, and the years draw nigh, when you will say, "I have no pleasure in them"' (Eccles 12:1). This passage does not suggest that the wildness of youth must be replaced by the mature spirituality of old age, but rather that youth is a particularly appropriate time to remember the Creator before the onset of old age presents so many problems that a man becomes preoccupied with mere survival. The call is not to become old, but to relate to God in an appropriate way for that particular age.[49]

The concept of maturity keeps cropping up in the New Testament. Paul wrote, 'Brethren, do not be children in your thinking; be babes in evil, but in thinking be mature' (1 Cor 14:20). There is a sense in which we are called to leave childhood behind. 'Shun youthful passions,' he wrote to Timothy (2 Tim 2:22). Titus was to 'urge the younger men to control themselves' (Tit 2:6). To the Ephesians Paul explained that Christ had given various gifts to members of the church,

> for the equipment of the saints, for the work of ministry, for building up the body of Christ, until we all attain to the unity of the faith and of the knowledge of the Son of God, to mature man-

hood, to the measure of the stature of the fullness of Christ; so that we may no longer be children, tossed to and fro and carried about with every wind of doctrine, by the cunning of men, by their craftiness in deceitful wiles. Rather, speaking the truth in love, we are to grow up in every way into him who is the head, into Christ, from whom the whole body, joined and knit together by every joint with which it is supplied, when each part is working properly, makes bodily growth and upbuilds itself in love (Eph 4:12-16).

He used the language of physical development, but he was addressing grown men. It was their *faith* that was to leave childishness and to grow up to full manhood.

It was Paul's object to 'present every man mature in Christ' (Col 1:28). It was the growth and development of faith that brought him satisfaction (2 Thess 1:3,4). The call to maturity implies that everyone's faith should be growing and developing towards 'the measure of the stature of the fullness of Christ', an ideal that will not be reached in this life.

There is a tension between two ideas. On the one hand, maturity is something which can be realized in this life; but on the other, that very maturity involves a constant desire to keep growing, to push on towards a goal which will not be reached until the next life. Paul wrote:

Not that I have already obtained this or am already perfect; but I press on to make it my own, because Christ Jesus has made me his own. Brethren, I do not consider that I have made it my own; but one thing I do, forgetting what lies behind and straining forward to what lies ahead, I press on toward the goal for the prize of the upward call of God in Christ Jesus. Let those of us who are mature be thus minded (Phil 3:12-15).

Maturity is not a static spiritual quality. It is dynamic. It urges us on. It tells us we are safe in the hands of the One who has made us his own, but it stirs up a great longing within us to become more like him.

This maturity will also involve a concern for unity (Eph 4:13, 15-16) and a doctrinal stability (Eph 4:14).

The writer to the Hebrews made the same call to maturity. He emphasized that this call began with a firm grasp of basic biblical doctrine:

> For though by this time you ought to be teachers, you need some-one to teach you again the first principles of God's word. You need milk, not solid food; for every one who lives on milk is unskilled in the word of righteousness for he is a child. But solid food is for the mature, for those who have their faculties trained by practice to distinguish good from evil. Therefore let us leave the elementary doctrines of Christ and go on to maturity, not laying again a foundation of repentance from dead works and of faith toward God (Heb 5:12-6:1).

If we are to call people to spiritual maturity, we must first lay a foundation; a foundation of the elementary doctrines of Christ—repentance from dead works, and justification by faith in God's mercy instead. The 'children, tossed to and fro and carried about with every wind of doctrine', whom Paul wrote about (Eph 4:14), were those who lacked this foundation and so could not go on to maturity.

The mature Christian knows the basic fundamental truths of Christianity and knows that he knows them. He knows what are the essentials and is equipped to detect 'the cunning of men . . . their craftiness in deceitful wiles' (Eph 4:14), as well as 'to distinguish good from evil' (Heb 5:14). In youth work the call to maturity will begin with the teaching of simple basic truths, which alone can provide the foundation on which to build a mature faith. Discussions on current topics in a youth group cannot by themselves lay a basis for mature discipleship.

The youth leader who wants to lead young people into maturity must build on the right foundation. The ignorance of the Bible among students at school today does not allow us the luxury of teaching theological fashions or our own doctrinal hobbyhorses. We have to teach the basic truths from which a young person can derive a Christian approach to the immediate problems of his or her life. The doctrine of creation and how it applies to work and to unemployment, or to sexual ethics, or to social justice, would be one example. Another might be our concern that young people should understand how they can *know* that they are saved, rather than in trying to get them excited at the idea of being saved. Secondary issues (which are often the ones that divide Christians from one another most strongly, like baptism or speaking in tongues) will provide no foundation for a mature faith.

The call to maturity will also include the call to suffer. The writer to the Hebrews made it very clear that 'the Lord disciplines him whom he loves, and chastises every son whom he receives' (Heb 12:6, quoting Prov 3). He explained this discipline as an experience of suffering like the punishment a father inflicts on his son out of his love for him. God loves men so much that he allows them to suffer, in order that they may become what they could never become without suffering. 'For the moment all discipline seems painful rather than pleasant; later it yields the peaceful fruit of righteousness to those who have been trained by it' (Heb 12:11).

The good youth worker cares for the young people, not with the love that seeks to shield them from the consequences of their mistakes, but with the love that seeks to help them to learn not to make mistakes. They cannot be shielded from suffering and grow into mature disciples.

All Christian discipleship involves pain. As we call young people to maturity, we will share this truth with them. We may present our youth club programmes as fun, exciting, up-tempo occasions when everyone laughs, but we must not forget to mention that if the club is to be true to Jesus everyone is also going to learn to cry. The cost and privilege of Christian discipleship go hand in hand.

The Bible does not encourage us to idolize the young nor to glorify the old, but it does challenge us to develop a concept of maturity. The Greek word Paul used—*teleios* (translated 'mature')—has the sense of complete, perfect, fully developed. We need to think through the idea of the 'mature sixteen-year-old', fully rounded in his faith, lacking nothing. That would be an ideal. But it will be the ideal towards which we call the real sixteen-year-olds we find ourselves working with. We do not call them to a twenty-year-old faith. We call them to a mature faith, appropriate to their own individual age and development, and we must be clear what that is.

This call to maturity comes to all disciples of Christ, but it has a special application to the young because it must be distinguished from a mere human call to maturity, to grow up in their personalities and intellects. The spiritual call to maturity is not a matter of chronological age. Every age can aim at maturity in Christ.

The discipleship to which all Christians are called is not one merely of enthusiasm and excitement. Jesus promised his followers the same reception that he himself had suffered (Heb 5:8). This picture is not welcome to a generation which has grown up in greater material affluence and with less parental control than any of its predecessors. Never has life in the West been more comfortable. Our civilization is 'creating adults who don't know what to do with delay, discomfort, discouragement, and disillusionment' (Ronald Hutchcraft). We should remember that Sigmund Freud defined maturity as the 'ability to delay gratification'.

We are called to follow a most uncomfortable Saviour. When we present to young people a 'Christianity without tears', full of immediacy and excitement, making many emotional demands but few practical demands, with a stress on 'full-surrender' rather than perseverance, we do them and the gospel a fundamental disservice.

Our picture of discipleship must be one of 'Christianity *with* tears'. It must allow for the fact that suffering is the rule and not the exception in Christian experience. It must include the virtues of endurance and faithfulness, obedience to authority, submission to parents, self-discipline and self-denial, if it is going to be honest to the New Testament and fair to our peculiar age. Jesus himself never glamorized the call to discipleship. When we lay aside appeals to youthful enthusiasm, we may still be surprised at the power that resides in the simple way of the cross.

We must be quite clear about the long-term nature of the Christian life. John Allan has written:

> Young people are fascinated by the idea of permanence, but in their volatile, fluctuating emotional state, they can't make it work; 'Tracey and Jason 2gether 4ever' carved on the side of a school desk is a brave statement of wishful thinking, rather than a sober calculation of the probabilities. When we ask them to give their lives to Jesus, the idea may appeal, but they will find it very difficult to imagine anything as long-term as a whole-life commitment. They need to be able to envisage what they're taking on; which is why the most effective teenage evangelism is not done in emotional appeals at late-night camp epilogues, or after stunning rock concerts, but in the continuing context of a regular group meeting, where the young person has the chance to see Christian commitment at close quarters over a long period, in the person of his group leader![50]

The normal period of contact between a youth leader and a young person is all too short. But discipleship is for life. The youth leader must have the maturity to let each young person go at his or her own pace, never forcing a crisis that God has not planned. It is striking that Jesus dealt with almost everyone differently.

While we endeavour to respond flexibly and sensitively to each individual we encounter, there are still clear priorities in our goals for them. There will be a primacy to teaching basic Christian truth effectively. How we do it will vary with the individual, but in every case we will strive to create a clear understanding of spiritual truths because that alone has the power to transform behaviour (Rom 12:2).

We will want to lead everyone to 'hands-on' experience of the Bible, so that, whatever their academic abilities, their minds are fully engaged with it. As Saward and Eastman wrote twenty years ago: 'The need for Christian teaching in youth groups is not an interesting topic for speculation—it is a crying need—and the lack of it is a matter of weeping and gnashing of teeth.'[51]

In reading these two chapters on the communication of faith, there may be those who have gained the impression that they are geared to a particular type of youth work (a church-based, nurture-group variety). That is not my intention.

If the principles I have outlined are authentic biblical principles of communication, then they have as much to say to Christians doing open youth club work and detached work. They may pose some hard questions for those doing such work, but then they also challenge the presuppositions of much church-based youth work as well.

The theology of communication I have tried to sketch out frees the detached worker from a success-orientated ministry, judged by numbers. It allows him to work in obedience to Christ in the small and obscure ways that the kingdom of God often comes into our world (see the parables of Matthew 13). It also compels him to open his life deeply to a few in order to proclaim Christ to them in word and deed. It forces him to recognize the priority of the gospel message itself, without which his love and his self-sacrifice will be of no lasting significance; and it does not allow him to evade the responsibility of bringing those he is involved with into living contact with a community of faith (see chapter seven).

In appealing for maturity among youth leaders, and stressing the need for patience and perseverance, I do not want to obscure for one moment the crying need for an urgent zeal to see young people converted. We must temper that zeal with wisdom and maturity, but we must not extinguish it. If I have overstated the sombre side of the case, it is out of an alarm that this note is missing today, but I strive for a balance—the zeal that can persevere. The secret of achieving this lies in being biblical not only in our goals, but also in our methods.

7

An Insignificant Minority of Old Ladies of Both Sexes?

Young people and the church

The dullest experience in the country?

> Like a mighty tortoise moves the church of God.
> Brothers, we are treading where we've always trod;
> We are all divided, many bodies we,
> Very strong on doctrine, but as for charity . . . !

Unflattering caricatures of the church abound. The Church of England probably tops the list for its contribution to the poor image of the church:

> Words cannot convey the doctrinal confusion, ineptitude and sheer chicanery of the run-of-the-mill incumbent, with his Thirty-Nine Articles in which he does not even purport to believe, with his listless exhortations, mumbled prayers and half-baked confusion of the Christian faith with better housing, shorter hours of work and the United Nations (Malcolm Muggeridge).[52]

But most manifestations of church life have played their part in creating a public impression either of frenzied irrelevance, or of monumental boredom ('The church is the dullest experience that we have in this country'—Noel Edmunds.)[53]

It is the young who feel this with the greatest intensity. There is a sharp fall-off in church attendance during the teenage years. Three out of four children aged thirteen who regularly attend Church of England services will have stopped going to church by the time they are twenty.[54]

In considering the relationship between young people and the church (in all its shapes and forms), this image of institutional Christianity as extremely tedious ('grimly spiritual persons devoted to the worship of sonorous generalities') or distinctly weird ('arm-waving fanatics with their eyes closed crammed into a huge tent') is an inevitable starting point. The outward forms of church life can appear very far removed from the everyday concerns of young people at the end of the twentieth century.

A Bible Society survey of people's attitudes concluded:

> The Church presents itself as fairly irrelevant and in need of a change of image. Nevertheless compared with other institutions (Gallup European Values study) people had more confidence in the Church than in parliament, the press or trade unions!

So a 'relevant public image' is not such a significant factor as it might at first seem. When the survey *Teenagers and The Church*[55] was published, *The Times* religious affairs correspondent wrote:

> Dr Leslie Francis, who conducted the survey, makes a curious prejudgment throughout his commentary on it, one no doubt unconsciously shared by the Youth Unit of the British Council of Churches, which sponsored it.
>
> It is that churches must try to attract and hold young people by a variety of techniques and devices: by the adults in the congregation adopting a 'welcoming' attitude, by clergymen being 'approachable', by encouraging 'friendliness' among young churchgoers themselves, by allowing 'participation' in services and other church activities.
>
> By implication, religion must be made 'relevant' and sermons must be 'helpful' to young people; the services should give an impression of 'life'. (Those are Dr Francis's key words).

The evidence collected by the survey itself indicates that the Free Churches are by far the best in these respects, and the Roman Catholic Church the worst. Yet the evidence also shows quite unmistakably that the Free Churches have the fewest teenagers, the Roman Catholic Church the most, and the most committed.

The Roman Catholic attitude to teenagers is distinctly 'take it or leave it', and eschews the manipulative methods regarded as self-evidently necessary in the Free Churches. It is at least possible that that is what appeals to teenagers about the Roman Catholic Church, and earns their respect.

It is roughly true that a serious enquirer who knocks on the door of the local minister is likely to find himself warmly welcomed in, on his knees within an hour, and signed up that day; one who knocks on the local presbytery door may be rather coldly told to come back in three weeks, then to be offered a daunting six months' course of instruction 'if you really mean it'.

The two approaches parallel the two churches' attitude to teenagers in the congregation: one communicates a kind of insecurity, the other self-confidence.[56]

If the Christian community is over-concerned about its image in the eyes of outsiders, it is set on a dangerous course. Christianity has always been an advertising agent's nightmare and whenever historically it has acquired a 'popular' image it has put its spiritual vitality at risk.

A church with an enormous popular appeal to the young at a superficial level would call for careful examination. If Christianity is true, and if God deals with individuals at various stages in their lives, then we would expect there to be more old people in the church than young. (The longer a person lives, the greater the likelihood that he or she will come to a knowledge of the truth.) The reverse would be far more worrying. It would suggest that Christian belief is something to be discarded as our wisdom and experience increase. There are less creditable reasons for the predominance of older people, but the common accusation that the churches are mainly filled with the old may actually be one encouraging indication of the truth of the gospel!

The decline in church attendance during the teenage years suggests that there may be an artificially high rate of church attendance among children. Congregations have often focused upon children in the neighbourhood as a suitable target for their evangelism with remarkably little attention either to the Bible or to commonsense.

While it is comparatively easy to build up a large children's work or Sunday School, research indicates that 95% of Sunday School children from non-church-going families are not involved in the church by the age of fourteen. Large Sunday Schools are not always an indication of a healthy congregation. Nor, as we have seen, does the Bible identify other people's children as an especially appropriate target for evangelism. They are no more and no less appropriate than their parents. All too often the church has ignored the parents in favour of the children. It has also been said that the churches have concentrated too much on trying to evangelize other people's children, and too little on helping Christian parents bring up their own children in the discipline and instruction of the Lord.

This distorts the age-profile of some congregations and produces an apparent 'failure' at the level of the youth work, when so many drop away again. On the other hand, as I have already suggested, the fact that Christianity is true will tend to shape the other end of the age-profile of the congregation. There is likely to be a preponderance of the old. That is bound to influence congregations toward caution and conservatism.

It is at this point that we encounter a more serious aspect of young people's disillusionment with the church. It is not only to those on the outside that the Christian community appears irrelevant. It is those who have a degree of commitment and who experience church life from the inside who face a greater problem.

The credibility gap between what young people feel the church *ought* to be and what it is, as they have experienced it, has reached the point where Christians under twenty-five and those over forty have little common ground. Hence the growth of a 'Christian youth sub-culture' sustained and serviced by a range of events and agencies outside the institutional structures of the churches (Michael Eastman).[57]

The success with which these events and agencies have worked along the particular age band on which they focus has tended to confuse their relationship with the local church. Consequently that relationship is often tenuous.

There are young people who accept Buzz, Spring Harvest, Greenbelt, a holiday at Lee Abbey, the latest Kingsway LP, or the most recent night of celebration at the Royal Albert Hall with unquestioning enthusiasm, but who find it very hard to work out their relationship to a group of Christian adults who do not share their musical taste and cannot live at their demanding pace. Some question the need to establish the relationship at all. They call in doubt our traditional concept of what a 'church' is, suggesting that college Christian Unions, or youth groups, or even youth-orientated events like Greenbelt or Spring Harvest may in some senses fulfil the biblical role of churches.

There is good reason for young people's disillusionment with much church life. Their criticisms of the Christian community deserve close attention—the caution with which we conduct our business, the traditional style of so much of our worship, our introverted obsession with our own administration and buildings, our blindness to the crying needs of the world on our doorsteps, our stubborn resistance to change, our failure to serve God with the zeal he deserves, our refusal to love one another and to work together for common goals— all this, and much more, rightly comes under the condemnation of the young. But we will not grapple with the real problem of young people and the church until we arrive at a clear picture of what the 'church' is.

'The winged thunderbolt of thought and everlasting enthusiasm'

The New Testament uses the word 'church' in two senses. There is the universal church, the invisible body of Christ, into which every believer enters at the moment of his or her conversion (1 Cor 12:13). The word *(ecclesia)* means 'the called out', 'the summoned out'. The characteristic Pauline usage is 'the church of God' (1 Cor 1:2) or 'of Christ' (Rom 16:16), and this serves to give the Greek term its special Christian meaning. The universal church is the people called out by God at his initiative.

With his massive commonsense, Martin Luther provided a simple definition of the church in this sense: 'Thank God, a child of seven knows what the church is: the holy believers and the lambs who hear their Shepherd's voice' (1537).

They are a building which he is constructing, and which will ultimately be beautiful (Eph 2:19-22). Each of them is a living stone which is being built into a spiritual house (1 Pet 2:4-5). They are organs of one body (Eph 4; 1 Cor 12; Rom 12), members of one household (Eph 2:19), and sons of one Father (Gal 4:4-7).

But, as a building under construction, the universal church is not yet beautiful or symmetrical. God's family does not always show brotherly love, or demonstrate the Father's perfection. There is a tension in the New Testament's teaching between what the church already is and what it is becoming. There is a sense of God's achievement in redeeming his people, and also a sense of anticipation of further development.

> But you are a chosen race, a royal priesthood, a holy nation, God's own people, that you may declare the wonderful deeds of him who called you out of darkness into his marvellous light (1 Pet 2:9).

> Rather, speaking the truth in love, we are to grow up in every way into him who is the head, into Christ; from whom the whole body,

joined and knit together by every joint with which it is supplied, when each part is working properly, makes bodily growth and upbuilds itself in love (Eph 4:15-16).

Even in this universal sense, the church is not yet perfect. Although she is a bride, who already belongs to the bride-groom, she is spoken for and loved by Christ not because she is spotless, but in order that she may become spotless:

Christ loved the church and gave himself up for her, that he might sanctify her, having cleansed her by the washing of water with the word, that he might present the church to himself in splendour, without spot or wrinkle or any such thing, that she might be holy and without blemish (Eph 5:25-27).

It is the eye of faith that sees what the church really is here and now, and what she will become in God's purpose. This is not outwardly visible. Every age has had problems with the outward image of the church. It has always been easy to score points at the expense of the visible church with all its ugly failings and hypocrisies.

However, if our youth work is not based upon this elevated doctrine of the universal church, it is not based upon the Bible. We must recapture G.K. Chesterton's vision of the church: 'Rushing through the ages as the winged thunderbolt of thought and everlasting enthusiasm; a thing without rival or resemblance, and still as new as it is old.'

The local tin tabernacle

The New Testament also speaks of the church in a local sense—'the churches in Galatia', 'the church of God which is in Corinth'. Locality is essential to its character in this sense. If *the* church is an invisible, spiritual body of all true believers, then *a* church is a local, all-age, all-class, all-type, community of such believers.

Wherever two or three believers gather together in the name of Christ, he is present with them and they are a part of *the* church (*ubi Christus, ibi ecclesia*—'where Christ is, there the church is'). But they are not *a* church. In the passage where Jesus made this promise (Mt 18:20), he made it clear that two or three believers by themselves do not constitute a church. If I have a dispute with my brother, I am to raise it first with him, then with two or three others, and only after that to 'tell it to the church' (Mt 18:15-17).

'Scripture does not support the idea that any small group of Christians who happen to be thrown together can be regarded as "a church".'[58] The Acts of the Apostles distinguishes between the parties of gifted Christians who accompanied Paul on his missionary journeys (and who are never described as a 'church'), and the communities of believers in the various towns they visited (who are described as 'churches').

Michael Griffiths has suggested ten distinguishing marks of the local church in the New Testament:[59]

1. Location

The word 'church' is usually used in association with a particular town or city, or even a house.

2. Organization

Paul's concern in the pastoral epistles for order in the local church (e.g. Tit 1:5) shows that it was to be organized, although the New Testament does not provide any uniform pattern for that organization.

3. Authority

Paul left Titus in Crete to 'amend what was defective, and appoint elders in every town as I directed you' (Tit 1:5). A congregation was to have elders in authority over it. Michael Griffiths points out that when Paul established Christian communities in the towns of Galatia (Acts 13 and 14), significantly the word 'church' is not used of any of these new groups of Christians in Galatia until we read, 'And when they had appointed elders for them in every church . . .' (Acts 14:23).

4. Discipline

The writer to the Hebrews exhorts his readers to: 'Obey your leaders and submit to them; for they are keeping watch over your souls, as men who will have to give account' (Heb 13:17). The leaders were expected to be sentinels and shepherds who would guard the flock from its enemies and care for its well-being. This would involve 'the corrective ministry of admonition to bring individuals to repentance'.

5. Initiation

Baptism would be administered in the local congregation (although it does not appear to have been confined to it in Acts).

6. Communion

The Lord's Supper was clearly a regular activity 'when you assemble as a church' (1 Cor 11:18-34).

7. Teaching

When he addressed the elders of the Ephesian church at Miletus on his way to Jerusalem, Paul strongly emphasized his teaching ministry among them:

> I did not shrink from declaring to you anything that was profitable, and teaching you in public and from house to house, testifying both to Jews and to Greeks of repentance to God and of faith in our Lord Jesus Christ . . . I did not shrink from declaring to you the whole counsel of God . . . for three years I did not cease night or day to admonish every one with tears (Acts 20:20-31).

8. Spiritual gifts

The exercise of spiritual gifts is spoken of in a strongly congregational setting in the New Testament (Rom 12; 1 Cor 12; Eph 4).

> It was in the context of the full congregation, which included '. . . husbands . . . children . . . slaves . . . masters', that all the gifts of

Christ to his church could be expected and exercised.[60]

9. Families

Paul's famous injunction to 'be filled with the Spirit' (Eph 5:18) comes in a clearly congregational setting ('addressing one another in psalms and hymns and spiritual songs' Eph 5:19) and leads straight (without any further main verb in the Greek) into a passage applying this teaching to the relations between wives, husbands, and children. Families are basic to the structure of the congregation. 'A group of students or any other youthful peer group cannot properly be a local church in a fully biblical sense until the group includes married couples with children.'[61]

10. Universal in membership

The local church is not to be a gathering of the like-minded. It is a summoned-out group. It exists because of God's activity, not man's choice. It must resist the temptation to become self-selecting in its membership.

> There is no such thing in the Bible as churches for rich men and churches for poor men, churches for intellectuals and churches for dunces. Local circumstances, as when different languages are spoken, may mean that the membership of a church cannot be fully representative of all races, classes and conditions of men. But as far as it is possible, a church must aim to be all-inclusive (see 1 Corinthians 1:11-13; Galatians 3:27-29).[62]

So, according to the Bible,[63] the church is both the invisible body of Christ and a series of local congregations throughout the world.

> As we look at the New Testament two main ideas emerge. The first relates to all the members of God's Kingdom gathered round the Lord Jesus Christ—a heavenly spiritual reality. The second refers to the local church whether the church in Corinth, Jerusalem, Antioch, or even 'the church in your house' as in Philemon. The emphasis here is on locality, a group of Christians

gathered together and reconvening on a continuing basis of commitment first as those who submit to the sovereign rule of God as Lord, and to one another as fellow members of the household of God or fellow citizens of the Kingdom of God (Tony McCarthy).[64]

We tend to put the two truths in this order, hinting at a priority of importance between them, but Donald Guthrie suggests that historically they may have emerged in the reverse order:

It is not surprising that the initial idea of the church was of local communities of believers meeting together in one place. The extended idea of a Universal Church which linked these local groups into one entity or body took time to develop, but is well attested in the New Testament period. It was a logical extension of the local community idea, for if individual members were knit together locally, the same principle would link together communities which were formed on the same basis.[65]

Quoting this passage Tom Slater makes the point: 'The local church, then, is the focal point of Christian community.'[66]

A real mixture

The idea of a universal body of believers does not cause many problems. It is when we face the truth of the local church that the problems arise, and they are problems we cannot escape. If young people are to join the body of Christ, they have to join a local community of believers. 'We all have to answer the same question and that is, "What is our relationship with the Church?" Because, like it or not, that's where Jesus is in the world today' (Robert Webber). However disagreeable—and disagreeing—local churches may appear, they are God's chosen way of working in his world. So it is with these local churches that we must grapple if we are to help young people in their faith.

In listing ten distinguishing marks of the local church in the New Testament, nothing was said about buildings. The New

Testament gives us no grounds for thinking that Christians met in any special sort of building, let alone in buildings reserved specially for such meetings. Howard Snyder wrote, 'Christianity has no holy places, only holy people. . . . It is hard to find biblical support for constructing church buildings' (*New Wineskins* p. 58). Its heritage of consecrated church buildings is a dubious asset to the spiritual life of the Church of England.

Nor does the New Testament provide a clear blueprint for the organization, or the leadership structure, or the pattern of initiation, or the form of discipline for the local church. But the idea of a church as 'any group able to be the body of Christ in a particular situation' does not do justice to its teaching. Such a group is part of the universal church, certainly, but it is not *a* church.

The local church must have the ten distinguishing marks, and in particular it must be a mixture. It will always tend to try to become a gathering of the like-minded. This danger is particularly relevant for youth work. John Stott wrote:

> The Church must . . . exhibit its multi-racial, multi-national and multi-cultural nature. There has been considerable debate in recent years whether a local church could or should ever be culturally homogenous. A consultation on this issue concluded that no church should ever acquiesce in such a condition: 'All of us are agreed that in many situations a homogenous unit church can be a legitimate and authentic church. Yet we are also agreed that it can never be complete in itself. Indeed, if it remains in isolation, it cannot reflect the universality and diversity of the Body of Christ. Nor can it grow to maturity. Therefore every homogenous unit church must take active steps to broaden its fellowship in order to demonstrate visibly the unity and the variety of Christ's Church' (The Pasadena Report: Lausanne Occasional Paper No. 1, 1977).[67]

If all the members of a church are too similar, it suggests that something is wrong. It may be a similarity in social class, or in age, or in educational attainment, or in financial status, or

even in psychological type (a church which draws its membership exclusively from those who enjoy an extrovert, ecstatic
and energetic form of worship is lacking something just as
much as a church whose members will only tolerate a with-
drawn, highly liturgical, non-participatory form of worship:
both are catering for only one sort of person).

The church, in both biblical senses, is a part of the content
of the gospel. If the gospel is for all men and all women of all
races, classes, ages and types, then the church must be as
universal in its scope. Each individual local church must work
towards that ideal. It must proclaim the barrierless gospel of
the New Testament, where 'there is neither Jew nor Greek,
there is neither slave nor free, there is neither male nor
female, for you are all one in Christ Jesus' (Gal 3:28). In the
same sense, there is neither young nor old.

Where a generation barrier appears in congregational life,
it must be resisted as stoutly as racism or snobbery. The idea
of 'youth churches' as a permanent expression of the Christian
community's life is highly questionable. If we abandon the
vision of a church without age barriers, we are discarding a
part of the gospel, just as much as if we accept there should be
different churches for different classes, races or skin colours.

We have seen that young people are today's church, not
tomorrow's, but we ourselves must be convinced of this; we
must convince them of it; and we must convince the rest of the
church of it. The body cannot function as it is meant to if any
part is missing. It is the function of each part not primarily to
judge or improve the other parts, but to be committed to them
in love.

The temptation to leave the adult congregation behind in
youth work is great. With their apparent conservatism and
hypocrisy, their spiritual compromise and worldliness, their
cultural irrelevance and social divisiveness, their love of
traditional patterns of worship and their resistance to change,
the youth worker is tempted to ignore them and to concentrate on the teenagers. The church will not adapt itself to meet

young people's needs, so we forget the church and create our own structures geared to the young.

The Bible does not allow us to do that. It reminds us continually of the unity that Christ and his cross bring to human life (Eph 2:16-22). Teenagers need adults and adults need teenagers. Unless a local congregation is striving to unite the conservative old and the radical young, it is failing to live up to its calling, and failing to proclaim the gospel of the upside-down kingdom to the world. 'Teenagers . . . need to be assured that diversity is not only acceptable but actually desirable in the Church' (Keith Olson).[68]

It is important to remember, of course, that every individual congregation fails. Every church is deficient. The New Testament nowhere suggests the possibility of a perfect church here and now. In fact, if the first-century church had in any sense been perfect, then most of the New Testament after the letter to the Romans would not have needed to be written. What we actually find in the pages of the New Testament is a divided, quarrelling, backsliding church, within which the New Testament writers exhort their readers to struggle to guard the gospel and hold on to the precious truths that bring spiritual life.

New Testament congregations were mixed. Paul's problems did not lie with the persecutions of the Roman authorities, but with Judaising and Gnostic influences which had already gained entry to the church. Nowhere do we find a passage attacking the secular authorities who imprisoned him, but his attacks on certain people within the local congregations are vehement—'Look out for the dogs, look out for the evil-workers, look out for those who mutilate the flesh' (Phil 3:2, or see 1 Tim 6:3-5; and in other New Testament writers: 2 Pet 2; 1 Jn 2:18-26; 2 Jn 7-11, etc.). In our thinking about the church we must not allow more idealism to creep in than we can find support for in the pages of the New Testament.

Learning to live with clerical thrombosis

We need a thoroughly biblical doctrine of the church as the basis for youth work. It must encompass that exalted vision of 'a chosen race, a royal priesthood, a holy nation, God's own people' (1 Pet 2:9), as well as the realism that sees the local community of believers as it really is, with all its present spots and blemishes, and warns us that membership is going to involve a measure of suffering and self-sacrifice. If the local church of the New Testament is an imperfect church, then we must equip young people to cope with that.

Too many of the young grasp one half of this teaching, but not the other. They are encouraged to have an exalted vision of the 'perfect' church in the New Testament, full of power and evangelistic zeal, and to compare their own experiences of church life most unfavourably with it. They are encouraged to see themselves as change-agents within the local congregation, and to see their task as judging that congregation and changing it.

We must teach them the whole picture. We must help them to understand that to change the church they must first learn to love it and to belong to it. We must remind them (and ourselves) that commitment begins at the point of disagreement. Commitment to the body of Christ involves commitment to certain things that I may not like and would not personally choose. I do not choose my brothers and sisters in Christ, but I am to love them and to be committed to them. This is a supernatural experience and it will have a supernatural effect. The world understands our criticisms of the church—it is our love for the church that puzzles and convicts it (Jn 13:35).

Loyalty to the church leadership is often a problem for youth leaders, but it is one way for them to model to their young people their commitment to the whole congregation. Loyalty is another quality that begins at the point of disagreement. While I am in agreement with the senior elder, or the pastor, or the minister, or the vicar, or the house-church leader, I am not being loyal to him. I am simply agreeing with him. I can only begin to show loyalty when we disagree. Young people are particularly sensitive to the sort of vibrations that a leadership team gives out. They probably know better than the youth leader himself how loyal or disloyal he is to the pastor.

Every worker in a local congregation has a sense at times of suffering from what Anglicans call 'clerical thrombosis' (a clot in the pulpit). It is how we handle those frustrations and disagreements that can make the difference between equipping young people for effective membership of the community of faith, or preparing them for a lifetime of complaining about their local church.

We have already discussed the fact that a 'normal' community of believers may well have a slight preponderance of the old (and there is nothing wrong with that in itself), but it will tend to incline a congregation towards traditionalism. We have to help young people realize that a 'tradition' has no existence except in the people who hold it dear. Traditions are people. When I long to overthrow those traditions, I am in danger of trampling on the fellow-believers who cling on to them. My commitment to those people as fellow members of the body of Christ has to be weighed in the balance against my dislike of their traditions.

There are traditions that directly contradict the commandments of God (see Mk 7:9)—which we must oppose—but there are also traditions that uphold God's commandments, and ones that are neutral. We have to learn to distinguish.

All too often in youth work the leaders are passing on to the young people their own irritation with certain aspects of their local church (for example, the style of worship). Sometimes the dissatisfaction does not begin in the young people themselves, but in the youth leader. We must take care over what we are teaching our young people by implication about the church.

We may be convinced that it is the fault of the adult members of the congregation that young people are alienated. We may be infuriated by the hide-bound and blinkered traditionalism of adults. It may well be right for a youth leader to lobby for all she is worth with the leadership to introduce a change into the life of her church, but it is almost certainly wrong for her to whip up dissatisfaction among the young people themselves. She has a far more important and a far more valuable truth to teach them: across all those divides of age and culture which split our world asunder, within God's church 'we are all one in Christ Jesus'.

As a youth group begins to grasp the full implications of this great truth, it is more likely to become an effective force for change within the congregation. People find change threatening. Old people are often uncomfortable with the thought of innovations in the life and worship of their local church. They may be frightened by the idea of dance or drama in a morning service, or (if they are Anglicans) having to greet one another at the 'peace' in a communion service. They are able to change only as their 'comfort zone' is enlarged to include the new development.

Young people, who invade the life of the local congregation with an open and loving attitude to adults, have a great way of expanding older people's 'comfort zones'—so that they find they can tolerate, and even enjoy, what had previously caused them to shudder. It is not that they have suddenly been converted to the idea of dance (or whatever) as a medium of worship, but they have come to know and to love the young people doing the dancing, and it is therefore acceptable for their sakes.

I recall one church where the youth group regularly arranged services for the adult congregation. There was the usual teenage attitude to such occasions—where they saw it as an opportunity to try to drag the adult congregation out of the nineteenth century, but it was always tempered by one remark at the planning meetings: 'We *must* sing a psalm as well. We can't stand them, but the old ladies love them.'

Those same old ladies would regularly pester the leadership of that church with the request: 'When are we going to have another youth service? With *guitars?* We can't stand them, but the young people love them.'

That is the authentic New Testament attitude to worship—all too rare in debates about worship in the local church. It is also the body of Christ in action. It is not a case of the cultural tastes of the old and of the young becoming homogenous. It is a case of each learning to sacrifice themselves for the sake of the other. That is what the local congregation is for; it is an opportunity for me to sacrifice my tastes for the sake of other people. The question is not: 'Do I enjoy singing this chorus?' but: 'Do others enjoy singing it?' Or: 'How can we change the worship to suit them (not me) better?'

It is only by teaching the biblical doctrine of the church in all its fullness that we can hope to arrive at this situation. We sell our young people short if we teach them anything less. At conversion, they have a desperate need to become full members of the community of faith. The local expression of that community may be very imperfect, but if we do not teach them how to relate to what is, their faith will die long before they can bring into being what is not.

The young often have a strong sense of how wrong it is that the different denominations are divided from one another, and a strong desire to do what they can to dismantle the barriers between churches. We must teach them to apply that ecumenical fervour to dismantling the barriers within our own congregations as well, and to begin with the prejudices and intolerance we find within ourselves.

We all long to see our congregations change, but we must not allow our young people to put changing the church above loving it. 'Only those who have come to feel a genuine love for the church will be able to confront it with its own faithlessness and call it back to its true vocation' (Jim Wallis).[69]

Scratching where they itch

So far I have applied this Bible teaching about the nature of the church mainly to young people, but if it challenges them to a new and sacrificial attitude to the older members of the congregation, it challenges the adults to bite that bullet as well. The late Robert Kennedy said, 'The gap between the generations will never be closed—it must be spanned.' That responsibility sits firmly on the shoulders of the adult congregation.

There is a need to educate the congregation as to how they can encourage young people to take their rightful place in the local church's life. Once again we must start from the Bible's teaching. For example, we must take Paul's picture of the church as a body seriously. Many are familiar with this picture (Rom 12; 1 Cor 12, etc.), and if they were asked to indicate how the youth work fits into the 'body', they would probably suggest that it is a limb—perhaps a very important limb, like the right leg. But if we think in this way we are losing sight of what the Bible is trying to teach us.

The 'body' is essentially an organic picture of the church, not a structural one. The different limbs and parts of the body are not different social or age groupings within the church (like the Over Sixties Club, the Sunday School, the Deacons' Court and the Men's Group). They are those with different gifts. Consequently the young people are scattered throughout the body, because they will exhibit many of the spiritual gifts (if not all of them), just as the adult members of the congregation do. Some of the church's best musicians, actors, organizers, givers, carers, evangelists, etc. may well be among its young people. (As we have already discussed, the primary evangelists for that age group are almost certainly the young people themselves.)

So we cannot consign the young people to a section of the church's life. We cannot treat the 'youth work' as a neatly self-contained unit which, with the right resourcing and servicing, will deliver mature Christian disciples into the adult congregation of the church on their twentieth birthdays.

Young people must be encouraged to take their proper place in the body by adults who have been taught what that place is and are committed to drawing young people into the whole life of their church. Granted that the majority of adults will have been Christians longer than the majority of young people, then it is only right that the adults should be expected to have the maturity to make the greater sacrifices, particularly in matters where personal taste plays a large part, like worship styles.

As adults we must give serious attention to the uninviting image of so many of our congregations for the young. While the public image of the church is relatively unimportant (as we discussed earlier), the initial experience of church life for young people *is* important. It must scratch where they itch. 'As it was in the beginning, is now, and ever more shall be' is not an appropriate slogan for the life of the local church. We must not give young people the impression that their local congregation is so resistant to change that when Jesus returns the last seven words of the church will be, 'We never did it this way before!'

The Christian life is about change, and change as we have seen is a community process. Individuals will not find it easy to change themselves within an institution that is highly resistant to change. Church leaders ought at least to dream radical dreams, even if their style of leadership is naturally cautious. Dietrich Bonhoeffer wrote:

> The Church is the Church only when it exists for others. To make a start, it should give away all its property to those in need. The clergy must live solely on the free-will offerings of their congregation, or possibly engage in some secular calling. The Church must share in the secular problems of ordinary human life, not dominating, but helping and serving. It must tell men of every calling what it means to live in Christ, to exist for others *(Letters and Papers from Prison)*.

The flexibility that can allow the possibility of radical change is a necessary qualification for church leadership. Where it does not exist, young people will have a sense of alienation from the authority structures of a church.

There must also be an engagement with the real problems of contemporary society. A congregation which has not given serious thought to unemployment, even in suburban areas today, is condemning itself to a degree of irrelevance in the eyes of the young.

Many churches are addressing themselves to the business of job creation. Of course they are not able to do this on a scale that will make a significant impact on national unemployment statistics, but they can provide a sign to the world that Jesus Christ cares about all of society's problems. The small church to which I belong in South London has been able, with very limited resources, to plant a community worker and his family on a GLC 'problem' estate in the area. Partnerships with a suburban and a North American church, and with the local authority, have made this possible. It is not a big thing in itself, but such 'mustard seed' projects are close to the heart of the young and capture their imagination and interest. They speak to them of a living organism, adapting, struggling, changing and relating to its environment. Other congregations are finding ways to pool their resources and to start more ambitious schemes to tackle the social problems around them.

Outwardly the church will always attract the ridicule of the world. Public attention will focus on its scandals and divisions and failings and feuds. (It has been caricatured as the 'army that specializes in shooting its own wounded, preferably after torture'.) But the young person who joins it must experience a living community, responding to its environment and making real provision for his needs. A part of that provision will be for peer group discipling and nurture.

That peer group once again!

While I have stressed the need for integration between all the age groups in a local congregation, the different groupings also have a need to meet at times by themselves. This is particularly true of the young people. There is a healthy balance to be struck between all-age activities in the local church and age-specialist activities. I will be looking in chapter nine at how to achieve that balance, and how to correct it when it tips over. At this point I only want to establish the fact that there should be such a balance, and young people's needs will not be met unless there are some activities provided specially for them.

In an earlier chapter I looked at the biblical balance between the corporate and the individual (see chapter four: pages 70 ff.). Our culture encourages us to over-emphasize the individual dimension of youth ministry, persuading us to see young people as emerging individual adults. The Bible corrects this balance, forcing us to communicate a fully-rounded faith with a powerful community dimension to it, which entails membership of a body of believers totally committed to one another and to their shared task in the world, because individually committed to the same Lord. So we have to take the peer group seriously, recognizing in evangelism and in Christian nurture that 'no man is an island, entire of itself'.

In unchanging societies, like those of the ancient world, old age is valued more highly than youth. In a rapidly changing society like our own, youth is prized above old age. The Bible teaches the value of both ages: 'The glory of the young men is their strength, but the beauty of old men is their grey hair' (Prov 20:29). Within church leadership it is appropriate for the younger to defer to the older: 'You that are younger be subject to the elders' (1 Pet 5:5). But each age has its own place and significance. Old age is to be respected: 'A hoary head is a crown of glory; it is gained in a righteous life' (Prov 16:31). Youth is to be rejoiced in: 'Rejoice, O young man, in your youth, and let your heart cheer you in the days of your youth' (Eccles 11:9).

As God values every age equally and deals appropriately with each one, so the life of the local congregation should make provision for the special needs of all the age groupings contained within it. This may involve a local church in linking up with other local congregations in order to mount a viable programme for young people.

Three levels of Christian life

The communal Christian life has been helpfully described as taking place on three levels: the cell, the congregation and the celebration. The cells of the New Testament would have been the Christians meeting in someone's house (Col 4:15), and the congregations would have been the gathering together of such cells for the Lord's Supper (1 Cor 11:18). Celebrations are less evident, but are hinted at in the concepts of the universal and invisible church, and in the worship of heaven (Rev 7:9). It is said that all Christians need to participate in the life of the church at all three levels.

The cell level

For many young Christians the cell will be the youth group or youth fellowship within their local church, but there may be situations where their local church life is so weak that even at this level a para-church structure has to be set up to provide a viable group. Christian youth work may have to be done across several congregations (possibly incorporating 'open' youth work projects as well) to provide a proper cell life for young Christians. Without this, for the reasons we have already discussed (in chapters four, five and six) neither youth discipling nor youth evangelism will be effective. Local church leaders with a concern for the young in their area may need to work together to ensure that this takes place—a strategy to which we will return in chapter nine (and we will look at the school or college Christian Union in chapter eight).

The congregational level

This will be that of the local church. For the strong biblical reasons we discussed earlier in the chapter this is the most important level. The congregation cannot be a peer group. To some extent it is certain to be a deficient and inadequate community, but as it is obedient to the gospel it will endeavour to include all ages, all classes, all races, and all types. Every believer should be committed to such a community.

It is important that young people are encouraged to grow out of their youth peer group into an adult group at the right stage. This will be assisted by a gradual exposure to the adult members of the fellowship. Such exposure will occur in the congregation, but it may be more effective if they are also encouraged to join an all-age cell group (perhaps a home Bible study).

The official ceremonies of admission into adult church membership (such as baptism or confirmation) are often held at too young an age to help the adolescent with this move from the teenage peer group to the adult fellowship. But the move is vital. Every youth leader should want to see his young people grow out of the youth group and into the adult church. He will want to give them every assistance to take the step. Formalized admission into adult church membership will be helpful, but only if it takes place at the right moment in each individual's spiritual development. For many young people, fourteen is still too young and confirmation or baptism at that age can be harmfully premature.

The celebration level

Beyond the congregation and the cell, there is also a need for the celebration. There were times in the life of God's people in the Old Testament when they assembled in large numbers.

On those occasions the festal shout may have been one feature of their religious life: 'Say among the nations, "The Lord reigns!"' (Ps 96:10). (See also Ps 89:15 and Rev 7:9-10). Clearly there were moments in the New Testament as well when large numbers assembled, as on the day of Pentecost—although there is not a lot of evidence that very large gatherings were a regular feature of New Testament church life.

Young people particularly appreciate the experience of being part of a large and united group at a celebratory level. Such events can play an important part in their spiritual lives. There are, however, certain inherent dangers in this level of Christian activity and we will end this chapter with a brief discussion of the role of para-church organizations (which normally organize these large scale events).

'If it's big, it's God'

Howard Snyder has developed a helpful thesis about para-church structures around the idea of wine and wineskins. The wine is the church in the universal sense, and the wineskins are all the organizational expressions of that spiritual organism. He lists denominations, associations, missions, agencies, schools, hospitals, seminaries, congresses, campaigns, federations, movements, publishing houses, committees, boards, etc. (*New Wineskins* p. 154). The wine is unchanging ('cross-culturally valid' as he puts it), while the wineskins must be constantly adapted to make them functional and relevant in every different society.

While his thesis does not, in my view, pay sufficient attention to the biblical emphasis on the local church, with its ten distinguishing marks, it does help us to see the role of the larger Christian organizations which, in one way or another, span many local congregations. It is their task to serve the church in both biblical senses and, therefore, to serve the local congregation in particular.

Local churches need the resources, support, advice and

shared wisdom available through para-church activity—whether it is the denominations, the inter-denominational societies, publishers, record companies, conventions, congresses, Christian arts festivals, national youth organizations, book shops, or whatever—but structures which work on this level are to *serve* the local congregation, not to dominate it. They are a supporting infra-structure, not a hierarchical super-structure.

Large scale celebration events for young people can only be organized at a para-church level. Para-church youth organizations have a role to play as visionaries and servants to the youth work of the local church. They may start fresh initiatives across the country to encourage and assist local youth workers. The youth work of many local congregations has benefited enormously from co-operative ventures, where small groups of teenage Christians have been built up by one another, but the leadership of the local church must be respected and not imposed upon. Unless we hold to a biblical order of importance in this area, there will be many problems.

There will be the problem of the maverick Christian worker, who likes to sit loose to the local church and to criticize it, but is careful to have no proper relationship to it. He is therefore not discipled by, nor does he let himself come under the authority of, the local congregation, and he is a spiritual danger to himself and to others. He is not an unfamiliar figure in Christian youth work.

There will be the problem of: where does God speak to his church? Where are the prophets, and how do they relate to the pastors? Does God speak in some special way at an event like Spring Harvest, but not in the local congregation? When a large and powerful organization decides to hold an event at short notice which overthrows the longstanding plans of a smaller organization, who is to decide which of them God was actually guiding? If it's big, it does not necessarily mean it is straight from God!

There will be the problem of where pastoral responsibility

and authority over young Christians lie. The Bible teaches that we are to submit to those who have responsibility for our souls: 'Obey your leaders and submit to them; for they are keeping watch over your souls, as men who will have to give account' (Heb 13:17). Exactly the same idea is specifically applied to young people at the beginning of 1 Peter 5. In other words the young are to submit to those who work among them and have spiritual responsibility for them, not to superstar preachers and bright-light organizations.

It is a mistake for the leadership of a para-church organization to expect from its teenage members a loyalty which ought to be directed to the local church leaders. The local leaders, on the other hand, should assume full responsibility for their young people.

The para-church organization must not look down on local church leadership, seeing itself as the trend-setter, God's prophetic voice to the youth work of the church, and local youth leaders must not look up to national organizations, assuming that their size automatically supplies them with the answers to the particular problems of a particular local church situation. The Bible reverses this relationship and teaches us to put the youth work of the local congregation above the para-church youth organization.

In concluding this chapter, it may be helpful to suggest some guidelines for organizations planning a para-church youth initiative. These are the questions they should answer:
1. What will this event (or whatever) do for the body of Christ? (i.e. What *effect* will it have? Not what is our motive in putting it on?)
2. Does it fit into the work of the church (a) nationally? (In other words, have we taken into account all other events that might clash or overlap? Have we consulted all other organizations that have a shared concern in this area?) (b) locally? (In other words, do local youth leaders want it? Does it take into account and assist their work?)
3. What effect will it have on the expectations and loyalties of

the young people involved? Will it help to integrate them into the worshipping community of local congregations?

4. Will it be sensitive to the emotional vulnerability of the teenager? Or will there be unhelpful pressure to create in the lives of the young people crises that have not been planned by God?

5. In the present situation, is it necessary? (Not 'Will it be successful?')

8

Apron Strings and Chalk Dust
Young people in the family and the school

Much of adolescence is spent either at home or at school, so those involved in Christian youth work need an understanding of the Bible's teaching on the family and on education. They play such an important part in the life of a young person that the youth leader must have a clear biblical perspective on them. As there is far more biblical material directly related to the family, I will start here and deal more briefly with the school at the end of the chapter.

God as Father

A Christian understanding of the family is important because God speaks of his relationship to his people most often in terms of a father and his children:

> As a father pities his children, so the Lord pities those who fear him (Ps 103:13).

> My son, do not despise the Lord's discipline or be weary of his reproof, for the Lord reproves him whom he loves, as a father the son in whom he delights (Prov 3:11-12).

> When Israel was a child, I loved him, and out of Egypt I called my son (Hos 11:1).

The Lord's Prayer (Mt 6) and the parable of the prodigal son (Lk 15) develop the idea. Jesus completed it by calling God 'Abba'—'Dad' (Mk 14:36), and teaching his followers to do the same through his Spirit (Rom 8:15-16).

We should not miss the point of this. While human fatherhood teaches us a little about our heavenly Father, it is more important that our heavenly Father teaches us much about human fatherhood (and motherhood). Paul wrote, 'I bow my knees before the Father, from whom every family in heaven and on earth is named' (Eph 3:14-15). Bishop Severian of Gabala commented on this in the fifth century: 'The name of Father did not go up from us, but from above came to us.'

It is sometimes said that to speak of God as a father is unhelpful, because so many people have unhappy experiences of their own human fathers. It is true that family life is under strain today, but the concept of God as a parent—he is sometimes spoken of in terms of motherhood also (Deut 32:10-12, 18; Is 66:12-13; see Lk 13:34)—is so central to the Bible's teaching about his revealed character that it cannot be ignored. In particular, it provides powerful guidelines for family life.

Conflict between the generations

Conflict and stress within the family is nothing new. The pace of change in our century has sharpened our sense of the distance between the generations, but the Bible too is concerned with the problem of the generation gap. The bumper sticker which reads: 'Get even—live long enough to become a problem to your children,' might well have raised a smile even in the society of ancient Israel!

There are specific examples of conflict between the generations, like King Rehoboam and his advisers. When he succeeded his father, Solomon, Rehoboam was challenged to predict the style in which he would rule (1 Kings 12:1-16). He consulted first his father's generation and then his own, and took the latter's advice ('My father chastised you with whips, but I will chastise you with scorpions') with disastrous consequences.

We have already considered the Bible's stress on the need for each generation to communicate spiritually with the next generation (chapter five). It also contains many examples of the failure to do so effectively.

Eli's failure with his own sons, Hophni and Phinehas, contrasted with his success in bringing up Samuel as a faithful servant of God (1 Sam 1-4). But then the same pattern set in with Samuel: 'When Samuel became old, he made his sons judges over Israel. . . . Yet his sons did not walk in his ways, but turned aside after gain; they took bribes and perverted justice' (1 Sam 8:1-3). David's spiritual stature as a man after God's heart was not communicated effectively to his children if Absalom was anything to go by. Even Solomon fell far short of his father's zeal for God.

Conflict within the family and between the generations is a consequence of the Fall (Cain and Abel, Gen 4), and will be a particular feature of 'the last days' (2 Tim 3:1-5). The Old Testament ends with a lovely prophecy of restored harmony between the generations: 'And he will turn the hearts of fathers to their children and the hearts of children to their fathers' (Mal 4:6). This prophecy is picked up and applied to the work of John the Baptist when the angel told Zechariah: 'He will go before him in the spirit and power of Elijah, to turn the hearts of the fathers to the children, and the dis-obedient to the wisdom of the just, to make ready for the Lord a people prepared' (Lk 1:17).

What the Bible has to teach about family life is realistic and relevant for an age like our own where the family is under attack. It addresses itself to the problem of the generation gap and promises us that it is God's purpose to resolve it (see Prov

17:6).

It might be helpful to review some of the particular pressures that Christians must contend with in their family life today. There are the social trends that I mentioned in chapters one and two: the demise of the extended family, the rise in the divorce rate, the increase in illegitimate births, the rampant materialism of Western society. Perhaps more significant is the enduring myth of marriage and the family in the popular consciousness.

By the time they reach forty, 65% of all women and 91% of all men have been married at least once. Apparently even the experience of marital breakdown does not destroy the dream since one third of all marriages involve the remarriage of one or both partners. Many people expect marriage to solve their deepest longings for personal fulfilment.

> The do-it-yourself reality kit that marriage and the family provide make them enduringly popular. As many people are getting married as ever, and those who get divorced usually remarry within a short time; even if the experience of marriage is unhappy, the *idea* of marriage is still believed in and people are willing to have another go . . .
>
> The creation of a home world and of a self-sufficient universe of meaning within the modern family is perhaps the prime way in which people in modern society protect themselves from the aloneness and lack of meaning that ensues from mankind's rejection of God (Tony Walter).[70]

Marriage and the family are part of the suburban dream in our society. We long to create a 'world of our own that no one else can share', as The Seekers sang. The family is thought to have a monopoly on the exercise of love, and to be the place of ultimate security.

Like most myths, this one relies on not being examined too closely in order to maintain its hold over us. While marriage and the family are for many their greatest haven, they may also be the greatest stress point. Statistically, the person any one of us is most likely to be murdered by is our own husband or wife!

The Bible makes it clear that family life will be tough. It is in the family that relationships are at their most intense. Samuel Butler commented, 'One of the surest signs of our Lord's extraordinary effect on people was that Simon Peter continued to follow him after he had healed Peter's mother-in-law!'

Order in the family

So the need for ordered relationships in family life is heavily stressed. The Old Testament law spelt out the severest consequences for a son's disobedience to his parents:

> If a man has a stubborn and rebellious son, who will not obey the voice of his father or the voice of his mother, and, though they chastise him, will not give heed to them, then his father and his mother shall take hold of him and bring him out to the elders of his city at the gate of the place where he lives, and they shall say to the elders of his city, 'This our son is stubborn and rebellious, he will not obey our voice; he is a glutton and a drunkard.' Then all the men of the city shall stone him to death with stones; so you shall purge the evil from your midst; and all Israel shall hear, and fear (Deut 21:18-21).

This punishment (inappropriately severe to our way of thinking) serves to indicate the importance of order in the home. Stoning for filial disobedience does not receive any endorsement in the New Testament, but the importance of children obeying their parents does: 'Children, obey your parents in everything, for this pleases the Lord' (Col 3:20; cf. Eph 6:1-3).

I have already argued that there is not a hierarchy in the home in the sense that the older generations are more important or more valuable than the younger ones (see note 49), but we are taught that there must be order in the home. A man who does not provide for his own family is worse than an unbeliever (1 Tim 5:8). When Paul instructs children to obey their parents, he immediately instructs fathers not to provoke or irritate their children lest they become angry and rebel (Eph 6:4), or become depressed and lose confidence in themselves (Col 3:21). Within the family there is a 'headship', a leadership in submission, accorded to the husband: a role which requires greater sacrifice and humility than that demanded of the wife (Eph 5:21-33).

It is the father's responsibility to see that the relationships within the home are well ordered. Discussing local church leadership in the pastoral epistles, Paul makes this clear: 'He must manage his own household well, keeping his children submissive and respectful in every way; for if a man does not know how to manage his own household, how can he care for God's church?' (1 Tim 3:4-5; see also verses 12-13; and Tit 1:5-6).

Paul here sets higher standards for church leaders than could be expected of every believer. Titus is instructed only to appoint elders whose children are believers. As we shall see, however good as a father and a husband a Christian man may be, he cannot guarantee that his children will also believe, but he can take responsibility for the ordering of his home life in obedience to God's will.

The correct order of priority is that the man must first put God in the centre of his own life. He then seeks to run his family according to God's will as revealed in the Bible. He does this primarily for God's sake, out of obedience to him. Adrian Rogers has written, 'I've been a pastor many years, and I have yet to see a home where the wife and children did not follow the man if he, from the beginning of the marriage, loved and served God.'[71] The man must focus first on God, and then on his wife and children.

The competitive materialism of our society with its distorted emphasis on the acquisition of possessions puts great pressure on husbands to pursue successful careers. The pursuit of a successful career, even if it does not bring financial rewards, confers status on a man and may provide him with considerable personal gratification. But this 'idolatry of the career' deters husbands from giving to their homes and families the time and energy needed to lead them in the way God requires.

The importance of family life

As we have seen, the home is not an easy place. The trials and tribulations of family life are obvious. The Bible does not encourage us to see it in any other way. The process of 'de-parenting', whereby a child gradually becomes independent of his or her parents (a process that starts at birth), is more painful for the parent than for the child. 'The parent must gain his freedom from the child, so that the child can gain his freedom from the parent' (James Dobson).[72]

Just when an adolescent in a family may be facing serious developmental tasks, as she moves out of the home into a peer group, her parents may be facing equally serious developmental tasks in maintaining a certain standard of living, parenting a teenager, developing adult recreational activities, adjusting to their own and their spouse's physiological changes, coping with aging parents. A family is a dynamic unit—every member is changing all the time. It is not just the children who develop while the adults are static and stable—fixed anchor points within the relationship. They have their own developmental tasks to contend with.[73]

The 'problem' of teenage children is sometimes also the 'problem' of parents facing their own mid-life crises. One mother was heard to say, 'The problem with my sixteen-year-old is that she behaves like a teenager!' Perhaps her daughter might have said that the problem with her mother was that she behaved like someone going through the menopause. There is nothing wrong with either the menopause or the teenage years, but those experiencing them have special emotional needs which will make special demands on family life.

Many men never channel into their family life even a tiny proportion of the time and energy that they give to their careers. This can be just as true of men in full-time Christian work as of those in a secular job (it is also true of some women). In fact, the more 'elevated' the job or vocation, the more likely it is to cause a man (or woman) to upset God's order for family life. Those in Christian work or in a caring profession (like medicine or social work) are most tempted to put the demands of their work above their calling to be husbands and fathers.

We can picture God's order of priorities as a series of concentric rings around the individual. The innermost ring represents his (or her) individual relationship with God, the next the relationship with the spouse, the third is the relationship with the children and with parents. Only after that comes a ministry to others. (For the single person there may only be a 'parents ring' between the personal relationship with God and wider ministry, which is why single people are so precious to the church—they have a capacity, while single, for wider ministry denied to the married.)

Now obviously there is overlap and interplay between each ring, but the point is that we cannot ignore these circles. We must approach youth ministry through the rings of our other responsibilities. We cannot jump them. If we try to bypass them, we jeopardize all our activity.

I will never get my relationship with my wife right, until I first get my relationship with God right. I will never get my relationship with my children right, until I first get my relationship with their mother right. If I am involved in youth work, I will never pastor young people properly until I first relate properly to my own children and my own parents. We are often sorely tempted, however, to use our ministries or our vocations as an excuse for sacrificing our marriages and our families. God does not mean us to do this, but neither does he want us to confine ourselves to the central rings. He means us to work out from them for the benefit of others.

The Bible does not present the family to us as a haven of security and pleasure, but it does provide us with clear guidance to give time and energy to how we conduct our family life. This is not a low priority. It is more important than our careers; it is more important than our standard of living; it is more important than the education of our children; it is more important than our ministries.

The pressures that oppose this Christian teaching are three-fold:

1. The myth of the 'suburban dream' which creates an unrealistic and harmful notion of domestic happiness, so that we are always chasing an unobtainable marital and family bliss. Marriage and the family will for many be the place where they experience their greatest happiness: they will also be the place where God teaches us our hardest and most painful lessons.

2. The quest for material possessions, which never tires of trying to deceive us that a man's life *does* consist in the abundance of his possessions. It substitutes material values for spiritual ones, so that we start to believe that the houses we live in, the cars we drive, the gadgets we enjoy, the decor we arrange, the possessions we delight in, the holidays we go on, the pets we keep, the toys we provide, will actually make a concrete contribution to the happiness of our family life.

3. The 'idolatry of the career' which persuades us never to question the work ethic of our jobs, so that an offer of promotion amounts to the word of God. It is not to be questioned on spiritual grounds—the effect it will have on our family life, on our friendships, and on our participation in the life of the church. 'The firm would not have asked us to move, if God had not meant us to'—we may not actually say it, but it is our unconscious thought process.

The dangers of determinism

If the Bible stresses the importance of family life and of ordered relationships within the home, it also provides a pattern for parenting. God is a Father whose first son, Adam, chose to disobey him. He did not then press the delete button and rewrite the script. He had made Adam in his own image and had granted him freedom and dignity. Adam expressed that freedom by disobeying his Father and they both suffered the consequences.

As parents, God calls us to be to our children what he is to us. We will not control what we bring into the world. Our children are not our pets; they are a temporary trust from God. They are much more than an extension of ourselves.

There is a mistaken belief today that it is the parents' job to create a desirable character and good habits in their child, and that any failure is due to parental mismanagement. This belief springs from the myth of 'determinism'—the view that every effect is the inevitable result of certain causes—and it removes from the individual the freedom and dignity which God has given to him or her. It also loads parents with guilt.

Experience tells us that good parents do not *always* produce good children and bad parents do not *always* produce bad children. Clearly there are a great many factors involved in the development of a personality. Heredity and environment play their part, but the Christian view of man will always assert the God-given freedom and dignity of each individual as well. I am not a helpless victim of my genes, my upbringing and my circumstances. I am a being created in the likeness of God with a will of my own, and with the ability to choose. Determinism would steal that from me.

Parents should not always feel guilty because their children do not turn out well, nor can they take all the credit when they do come up trumps. But determinism and the competitive nature of Western society will be urging us to do so, telling us that the younger generation is our most reliable status symbol.[74]

We are not given our children by God so that we can boast of their good points or be ashamed of their failures. John White's basic rule of parenting is: 'As God is to me so must I be to my children.'[75] Our aim is to be godly parents, not successful social scientists. We will go astray if the question uppermost in our minds is: 'How can I rear my children successfully?' That has only one answer: 'I cannot, because they are not my products.'

However, if my question is: 'How can I be a good parent?' then the answer is: 'As God is.' So I do not try to be a good parent for my children's sake, but for God's sake. As a Christian father, I keep an eye upon my heavenly Father and I try to conduct myself according to his will, not according to what I hope the effect will be in the life of my children. I trust that result to God.

The search for personal worth

So I must try to allow my children the freedom and the dignity that God grants to me. Parents allow their children increasing freedom to choose, not because they don't care about them, but rather because they do care. They accord them dignity and respect by allowing them an increasing freedom within the order of a Christian home, because God accords dignity and respect to mankind.

The home plays a vital part in building up the self-esteem of a child. God makes it clear that he values every human being highly—not just by creating them in his own image with freedom and dignity, but also by sending his own Son to die for them: 'You know that you were ransomed from the futile ways inherited from your fathers, not with perishable things, such as silver or gold, but with the precious blood of Christ, like that of a lamb without blemish or spot' (1 Pet 1:18-19). Human parents have the task of instilling personal worth in their children, and it is not a task that can be delegated.

Dr James Dobson has written: 'Personal worth is not something human beings are free to take or leave. We must have it, and when it is unobtainable, everybody suffers.'[76] There is often a link between irresponsible sexual behaviour and low self-esteem. Adolescents with the greatest sense of inferiority are those most vulnerable to sexual experimentation and exploitation. 'Lack of self-esteem produces more symptoms of psychiatric disorders than any other factor yet identified.'[77]

James Dobson suggests that there are two coins of human worth in Western society. The golden coin is beauty. 'The most highly valued personal attribute in our culture (and in most others) is physical attractiveness.' We reward the attractive and penalize the ugly from the earliest days of life. Significantly, most of us do not think we are good-looking. Particularly during the growth spurt of puberty, young people are highly conscious of their looks. One study of two thousand teenagers asked the question, 'What do you most dislike about yourself?' Skin problems outranked every other reply by a wide margin.

The silver coin of human worth, according to Dr Dobson, is intelligence. The development of universal education in the West has given academic ability social prominence. For many young people, however, their time at school is one long painful assault on their self-esteem. Parents are concerned to know whether their child is above or below the average of the class. 'We know by the distribution of intelligence that one fourth to one half of our children will eventually enter adult life having had twelve years' experience in feeling dumb.' Dobson advises parents to de-emphasize academic achievement as a value in the home (it is not, after all, something that God rates highly), and to help the slow learner to find his compensating skills.

The Bible teaches that family life at home should be regulated in such a way that each member can discover their own worth and so build up their own confidence. The Living Bible's translation of Ephesians 6:4 is:

> And now a word to you parents. Don't keep on scolding and nagging your children, making them angry and resentful. Rather bring them up with the loving discipline the Lord himself approves, with suggestions and godly advice.

The parents' task within the family is to shape the child's will, but also to preserve (and strengthen) the child's spirit. (Many of James Dobson's books contain valuable advice on this aspect of parenting.)

This task is particularly important during adolescence (when the urgent search for identity can create a crisis of self-confidence), although it must start long before then. The only age group in American society today with an increasing death rate is teenagers. This is largely due to the incidence of suicide. Attempted suicides are more common among teenage girls, but teenage boys succeed more often. It is God's purpose that there should be ordered relationships within the home in order to allow the young to grow up with a strong sense of their own value.

Lessons for youth ministry

Anyone working with young people needs a Christian understanding of how family life should work. This is, first, because we must get our own family life on sure foundations.

As we noted earlier (p. 165), Eli was an example of someone who was much better with someone else's child, Samuel, than he was with his own children, Hophni and Phinehas (1 Sam 1-4). It is a pattern that is all too familiar in Christian youth work, but notice what then happened to Samuel: he himself judged Israel justly, but when his sons, Joel and Abijah, succeeded him as judges in Beer-Sheba, they 'did not walk in his ways'. 'They took bribes and perverted justice' (1 Sam 8:1-3). It was Hophni and Phinehas all over again.

Eli had shown Samuel how to walk uprightly himself, but he had never shown him how to bring up his own sons in the fear of the Lord. He had not provided Samuel with a model of godly parenting. Neither of them as fathers could have forced their sons to be godly, however much they desired it, but they both revealed their weakness and inadequacy as parents by allowing their ungodly sons to succeed them as priests and judges over Israel. Moreover that pattern of weak fatherhood was effectively communicated from Eli to Samuel.

So a proper understanding of, and obedience to, God's order for the family is a prerequisite for Christian youth work. Two of the most helpful books for the youth worker widely available today are both actually about the family: *Hide or Seek* by James Dobson (Hodder & Stoughton 1982), and *Parents in Pain* by John White (IVP 1979). They contain tremendously useful teaching about youth work and I have drawn heavily on them both in this book.

Much damage can be done in youth ministry by well meaning people who have not yet worked out God's order of priority in their own lives. We must not sacrifice our families or our marriages for the sake of our ministries. We cannot teach others to obey the fifth commandment unless we show a proper respect ourselves to our parents. Otherwise we may sow a disastrous harvest in the lives of the young people we work with. We may endeavour to teach the Bible faithfully, but our lives will be contradicting it. What we model with our lives will probably prove more influential in the long run than what we say with our Bible-teaching programmes.

The fatherhood pattern

There is another solid theological reason for grounding youth work in an understanding of parenting. This is that God has provided a pattern for our theological understanding of him by calling himself a Father.

As we have seen, this is the way his relationship with us is most often expressed. It gives us an understanding of why we are permitted the freedom to rebel against him, to spoil our lives and to destroy his creation. It also helps us to grasp the liberty of the sons of God: once our relationship with him has been restored through Jesus (when we forsake our rebellion and accept forgiveness because Jesus died in our place to take the consequence of that rebellion), then we start to grow up into 'adult' children.

This not only shows us how we ought to behave as human parents, giving freedom, dignity and self-respect to our children. It also has important lessons for youth ministry. We must grant to young people the same dignity and respect that God accords to all people.

On the one hand, God allows his children to rebel. He does not withdraw their freedom at the moment of disobedience. Although he paid the highest price to obtain our salvation, he never violates the integrity of the person who chooses to turn away from him and to spend eternity apart from him in hell. With infinite sadness he endorses that choice, turning his own eyes away (Hab 1:13), giving that person up (Rom 1:24, 26, 28), and forsaking him as he has forsaken God (Mk 15:34).

One of the hardest experiences in youth work is to learn to let a young person go; to let him make mistakes, to reject Christ if he chooses to, and to desert the fellowship. There is a strong temptation to use every means, fair or foul, to hold on. Emotional pressure from a well-intentioned adult can easily violate a young person's integrity. But if God lets people go, so must we.

He stands outside time (2 Pet 3:9). His schedules are not always ours. We can precipitate a spiritual crisis in the life of a young person which God never intended to happen then. It may be our task just to sow. God will provide an Apollos to water, and perhaps someone else to reap (1 Cor 3:6-9). He will certainly never overthrow a young person's freedom of choice. He is the One who does the work and decides when it is to be done.

On the other hand, in our relationship with God as 'adult' children we have a different liberty. The fundamental Christian response to God is faith not works, liberty not law-keeping. It is the liberty to do right out of gratitude. We live under grace and by faith. Day by day we have to explore which of various grey options is right for us now.

So in youth work we have to help young Christians to cope with a world in which issues are rarely black or white. For the young person legalism is all too easy and it is often the immature Christian response. There are clear biblical principles, and we have the presence of the Spirit to guide us as free sons and daughters, but there is no set of rules to pass on. The Christian life is essentially a relationship of love. Our ultimate moral authority is a Person and not a principle.

It is the youth worker's task to help young people make this transition in a culture which stresses no rule except self-fulfilment: 'If it feels right, do it.' We have to wean them away from that without encouraging them into legalism on the one hand or a weak 'situation ethics' on the other. The Christian does not just weigh up each situation on its merits. There are fixed biblical principles, and, above all, a clear moral authority in the Person of Christ. But it is not always easy to discern his will. We will not always get it right. The mature Christian is prepared to wrestle humbly with complicated issues, trusting God's grace more than his or her own moral ability. It is only the immature who claim certainty in areas (like pacifism) where Bible-believing Christians have disagreed for centuries.

Blood thicker than water

So the pattern of fatherhood that God provides is important both for family life and for youth work. In fact, there is a considerable overlap between the two.

The cultures of the Old and New Testaments presuppose a large extended family. More normal in our society is the nuclear family of parents and a couple of kids, possibly separated by some distance from the nearest relatives, and possibly fractured even further by marital breakdown. We find it hard to understand now the sense of corporate solidarity that was present in the Old Testament family. The people of Israel did not question God's justice in visiting 'the iniquity of the fathers upon the children and the children's children, to the third and fourth generation' (Exod 34:7). They accepted a corporate dimension to human life, which is alien to us.

I have already discussed the biblical balance between corporate solidarity and individual responsibility, and how it relates to the conversion of a young person (chapter four p. 70 f.). We saw there how our cultural world view predisposes us to exaggerate the individual at the expense of the corporate. We need to correct that balance, particularly if we want to understand how the young person relates to his or her family.

Each young person is a part of his family background, however shattered that family may be. In some cases there may be a sense in which God is visiting the iniquity of the parents upon children and children's children, and we will never fully understand the individual until we first understand that. Without falling prey to the myth of determinism, we can allow that each person is at least partly the product of their family background.

The Home Office conducted a survey of teenage delinquency and family backgrounds in 1983. One third of all offenders dealt with by the criminal justice system are under seventeen years old. The peak age for officially recorded offending is fifteen for males and fourteen for females. About 160,000 juveniles a year are found guilty or cautioned for indictable offences.

With these juvenile offenders the two most important factors relating to delinquency were found to be friends and family. The report (in the *Research and Planning Unit Bulletin*) said, 'The contribution to, and cost of, crime by young teenagers when they are still very much part of the family and still at school is enormous.'

Ten years earlier the Headmaster of Eltham Green School had written to *The Times*:

> The children who present disciplinary problems in school and who get into trouble out of school usually come from unsettled home backgrounds. It is almost unknown in my experience for a child from a properly loving and caring home where there are two

parents to descend into delinquence. Never was it more true than it is today that the sins of the parents (including their not being together) are visited upon the children.[78]

Some young people are trapped in a cycle of sin and deprivation that distances them from Christian morality. When the church allows middle-class culture to affect and distort Christian morality, it makes the gap appear wider still. Other young people from different social backgrounds are trapped in a cycle of acquisitive materialism that distances them from Christian morality too. That gap is not so obvious (because materialism is quite compatible with certain outward forms of church life), but it may be just as hard to cross with the gospel.

Of course, family background may have a quite different effect. Abraham's offspring were to enter into the benefits of the covenant that God made with their ancestor (Gen 17:7-8). It was an agreement made not just with an individual, but with his descendants who were considered present in the person of their forefather. The father's relationship with God benefited the children for many generations to come.

There is an interesting reference in 1 Corinthians 7:14, where Paul is dealing with the possibility of divorce when one partner is a Christian and the other not: 'For the unbelieving husband is consecrated through his wife, and the unbelieving wife is consecrated through her husband. Otherwise, your children would be unclean, but as it is they are holy.' Our strong Western individualism does not find it easy to make sense of such verses. For that very reason they probably have all the more to teach us. The unions between husband and wife and between parents and children are so strong that they must be taken into account on the spiritual level.

So Christian youth work must recognize this corporate solidarity. It does not negate the autonomy which God has granted to the individual, but it does balance it. So when dealing with a young person, the Christian worker is dealing with a family (however depleted or remote) as well.

The Bible does not allow us to regard our work simply as a series of case studies of individuals. In every case we are involved with the family too. In entering into a relationship with an individual we have entered into a relationship with her family. We have incurred certain responsibilities towards that family.

Christian youth workers have to work out what this means in practice, but they will certainly want to visit the homes and to establish a relationship with the families of their young people. If they do not, they are failing to grasp what the Bible teaches about humanity.

There will, therefore, be a big difference between dealing with young people from a Christian background and those from a non-Christian background. It may not always be easy to judge accurately how Christian any particular home is, but it will always be valuable to discover whether Christian values are being affirmed or denied in a particular young person's home life.

The young person from a Christian home

If the home is a Christian one, it will be one of the most effective means of discipling that young person. If the Christian faith is caught as much as taught, then the most powerful place for that is the family. Communication goes on in the family even when no one is talking. Whether we like it or not, our value system is being steadily transmitted to our children. They may neglect it, but they certainly know what it is— perhaps even better than we do ourselves!

The Old and New Testaments both take for granted that the normal context for the nurture of the young in the faith was the home and the family. We have already discussed passages like Deuteronomy 6:4-9. After the visit to Jerusalem, Jesus himself returned home to Nazareth and was obedient to his parents and 'increased in wisdom and in stature, and in favour with God and man' (Lk 2:51-52). We have no examples of second generation Jewish Christians in the New Testament. The nearest would be Timothy, and we know he learned from his mother and his grandmother, presumably at home (2 Tim 1:5; 3:14-15).

The home is certain to be powerful in discipling, but faith is not hereditary. The Proverb which says, 'Train up a child in the way he should go, and when he is old he will not depart from it' (Prov 22:6) is a general statement about how family relationships normally work. It is not a promise or an inflexible law. The book of Proverbs is aimed at children as well as parents—both have their parts to play.

Moreover, that verse is not only referring to a 'way' of good behaviour.

> The training prescribed is literally 'according to his (the child's) way' implying, it seems, respect for his individuality and vocation, though not for his self-will . . . the stress is on parental opportunity and duty (Derek Kidner.)[79]

Parents are to help their children to develop according to their own particular bent, as God meant them to be, by affirming what each child is. But, however well they do it, they will not be able to ensure that each child believes.

Indeed, they will want to be cautious that the de-parenting process does not lead to a natural rejection of the parents' faith in the teenage years. As a young person moves out from the family, he will naturally want to question and test beliefs he had previously taken for granted. The teenager becomes aware that he does not have to grow up like his father. In his search for his own identity, he may try on other adult identities to see how he likes them. Part of that search may well entail trying out a different set of standards and values to those experienced at home.

Growing up is a good and natural experience. The exploration and testing of values and beliefs is important because it is the main way a young person appropriates them for himself. The Christian family must allow for this. It is here that parents and youth leaders can work together.

The youth leader will know that Christian values are probably being communicated more effectively at home than at the youth group. More to the point, they *have been communicated* for many years. On the other hand, the young person may be badly in need of other Christian adults to relate to, rather than just his own parents, so that he can try on other identities and distance himself from the family life without having to reject the family faith as well, in his search for his own individuality.

The problem of the PK

There are special problems where a particular family is very deeply involved in Christian service. Americans have a term for such problems, they talk about 'PKs' (Preachers' Kids). Many of us will know the truth of Murphy's Law for Sunday School teachers—'Once a Sunday School class is set in motion, all disturbances originate with the minister's son.'

In these families there can often be resentment among the children that so much of their parents' time and energy seems to go on the life of the local (or wider) community of believers. Rightly or wrongly (perhaps too often the latter), the family has had to make sacrifices for the sake of the father's, and possibly the mother's, ministry. They may feel that they never have their father to themselves, that they are always having to share him, and that they have to compete with other pastoral concerns for his attention.

It is vitally important that the children of such families build strong relations with other Christian adults. They must see the faith modelled by other grown-ups, to whom they are well disposed, and who are quite separate from their families.

Perhaps in a sense the fellowship owes it to such families to take special care with their children. The fellowship has benefited from the time and energy that the parents have given in ministry to other Christians. The church can now recompense the children by the youth leaders giving extra attention to them.

So often the opposite is the case. Our attitude can be, 'He's just the pastor's son'—so he's not a very important part of our planning for the youth group, because, after all, he's going to get it all at home anyway. Or we may let ourselves think that youth work which is confined to the children of church families is in some way spiritually inferior to youth work which is designed to reach outsiders. We have no biblical grounds for thinking that.

Our priorities probably ought to be the other way round. All local church-based youth work ought to start with the children of the families who already attend the fellowship, because if we cannot nurture our own children properly in the faith, what is the point of trying to win other people's children? Our goal must be towards getting disciples, and not just decisions.

On top of that, Christian parents *need* the help of other Christian adults when their children become teenagers. Vicars, pastors, ministers, and full-time Christian workers of all sorts particularly need the help of the rest of the fellowship in bringing up their teenage children. However well-ordered the Christian home, the children within it will always benefit from developing relationships with other adult Christians during adolescence. This need is increased by the nuclear family which does not contain the Christian uncles, aunts, grand-parents and older cousins who might have been present in an extended family.

Special care

So the wise youth leader will think carefully about the special needs of young people from Christian homes, particularly from homes where a parent is involved in full-time Christian work. These young people may well have grown up believing, and be unable to look back to a period of their lives when they were conscious of not being Christians. Like Timothy, they may have taken in the Christian faith with their mother's milk and 'from childhood . . . been acquainted with the sacred writings' (2 Tim 3:15).

A heavy stress on the need to be converted and to have a 'before' and 'after' testimony will not be helpful to them. In their case, it is not making a decision for Christ, but working out what it means to follow Christ day by day, that is important. They will need help in developing their faith to keep pace with their physical and mental development. As they discover each new power and ability, it has to be handed over to the lordship of Jesus, or they will find themselves facing adolescence equipped with a Sunday School faith.

Of course, there are also those who grow up inside a strongly Christian home but who have never found a personal faith in Jesus for themselves. For them, Christianity is just an outward show with which they are over-familiar. They know only too well how to act out the part. The wise youth leader will want to bring them to their own point of personal decision, getting them to see that they cannot expect to cope with life (and death) on the strength of a second-hand faith.

Sometimes a young person from a Christian home asserts her individuality by expressing her faith in a markedly different way from the way her parents express theirs. She may choose to join a different fellowship or denomination. Her parents may find this painful and may need help in coming to terms with it.

Above all, the leader will need Spirit-given discernment and humility to identify the young person's particular needs and to endeavour to meet them. It will require a sound and mature theology which does not have to see each young person jump through an identical hoop of conversion, but which does have a passionate concern that they should each individually accept Christ's lordship for themselves and learn to live it out in every part of their lives.

It will be clear from what has already been said that the youth leader needs to support the Christian parent. He may want to encourage the church leadership to include regular teaching on Christian parenthood for the whole congregation. Many parents are desperate for support and instruction in this task for which modern society (by removing the extended family) has prepared them so badly.

The youth leader will certainly want to have good lines of communication with the Christian parents of his young people. He will keep them informed of the teaching programme as well as of the activities of the youth group, so that they can pray intelligently for what is happening. He may want to enlist their help with transport, hospitality, or funds. If he does so, he will usually find them extraordinarily well disposed towards what he is doing for their teenage children.

All the time, however, he will recognize that his role is a secondary and servant one. Under God it is the Christian parents' task to nurture their children in the faith. The youth group leader's task is to assist that, never to supplant it. He will encourage parents to fulfil their rightful role, offering help and counsel. He will resist every temptation to look down on parents, or to teach their children to do so (however much it might curry favour with the young people, particularly in their negotiations with authoritative Christian parents).

On their side, wise Christian parents will give their church's youth work all the support they can. They will appreciate its importance in the life of their own children. They will look for ways to support it practically and financially, and to press its case with the adult leadership of the church. They too will resist any temptation to be disloyal to their local congregation making sure that 'roast pastor' does not become one of the regular courses at Sunday dinner!

The church as family

It may be worth noticing at this point that there is a sense in which the Old Testament extended family has been superseded by the church. The Old Testament put great emphasis on religious instruction within the family. As we have seen, the only 'youth leader' it seems to know anything about is the parent. Jesus' teaching widened the concept of family:

> While he was still speaking to the people, behold, his mother and his brothers stood outside, asking to speak to him. But he replied to the man who told him, 'Who is my mother, and who are my brothers?' And stretching out his hand toward his disciples, he said, 'Here are my mother and my brothers! For whoever does the will of my Father in heaven is my brother, and sister, and mother' (Mt 12:46-50).

Jesus introduced a new community to the world, a community inspired by loyalties stronger than those of kinship:

> I have come to set a man against his father, and a daughter against her mother, and a daughter-in-law against her mother-in-law; and a man's foes will be those of his own household. He who loves father or mother more than me is not worthy of me; and he who loves son or daughter more than me is not worthy of me; and he who does not take his cross and follow me is not worthy of me (Mt 10:35-38).

It is not surprising that Paul picked up the terminology of the family and applied it to the church:

> I do not write this to make you ashamed, but to admonish you as my beloved children. For though you have countless guides in Christ, you do not have many fathers. For I became your father in Christ Jesus through the gospel. I urge you, then, be imitators of me. Therefore I sent to you Timothy, my beloved and faithful child in the Lord, to remind you of my ways in Christ, as I teach them everywhere in every church (1 Cor 4:14-17).

In fact, fatherhood is Paul's favourite picture for his own discipling: 'For you know how, like a father with his children, we exhorted each one of you' (1 Thess 2:11).

The mandate laid on the family by the Old Testament to pass the faith down the generations is now extended to the church. Race and family by blood are replaced in Christ by the church as the Christian family. Within that wider family, some of the tasks of the parent may justifiably be transferred to other adults. So there is here a special place for the teenage peer group, led by adults other than the teenagers' parents, within the life of the local church.

Clearly, however, the family was still important in the New Testament church. Jewish Christian children would almost certainly have been taught the faith within the family. We have already referred to the case of Timothy, who was a second (or third) generation Christian—it would appear from Paul's second letter to him that he learned the faith at home from his mother and grandmother (2 Tim 1:5; 3:14-15). But then, of course, the local church might have met in his home, so there was not the clear division we know now between what happened 'at home' and what happened 'in church'.

I do not know of any example in the New Testament or the first centuries of church history of a teenage peer group under Christian instruction, but that does not rule out youth fellowships now in our very different culture. Formal academic education has now been transferred from the home to official institutions. This is a cultural development, but it may indicate that a similar development in Christian nurture is appropriate for the sake of cultural relevance.

A more telling argument for the development of youth fellowships is the way the Old Testament concept of the family is extended to the community of believers, so that some of the activities of the family are now rightly transferred to the wider family of the church.

It would be wrong, however, to use this argument to play down the importance of the home. Many of the New Testament passages we have already looked at in this chapter make it clear that the home and the family are vital (Lk 2:51-52; Col 3:20; Eph 6:1-3; 1 Tim 3:4-5; 2 Tim 1:5, etc.).

The young person from a non-Christian home

There are all sorts of reasons why people today need extended families. The church's ability to provide such a family (particularly one bound together by supernatural love) is something that makes it specially relevant to our culture. The young person from a non-Christian home background is someone who will need a Christian 'family' as well.

With this sort of young person, Christian youth work has to recognize that the home (where the most powerful communication about values is likely to go on) will be pulling in a different direction from the gospel. It will stand for something quite different: perhaps for standards of honesty and sexual behaviour that are disobedient to God; perhaps for the good works of a man-centred 'religious' outlook—Eastern, humanistic, or pseudo-Christian; or it may just be an indifference to spiritual things, whereby Jesus Christ is nice enough in his own way, but he is not important compared with making money and the pursuit of personal well-being.

The influence of that background must always be considered while caring and praying for such young people. The youth leader can easily underestimate the ignorance they may have of the gospel. They may have no knowledge at all of the Bible and a very distorted view of what happens in Christian worship.

Here we have got to start at a very basic level of Christian teaching, taking nothing for granted. Both in evangelism and in discipling a foundation must be laid of the simplest spiritual truths—'Of repentance from dead works and of faith toward God' (Heb 6:1). It is possible for a young person to build the superstructure of an apparently genuine conversion and an apparently healthy Christian life without actually having laid the only foundation on which they can safely be grounded. This situation is more probable in the case of a young person from a non-Christian background.

There may be great pain in that background too. It may be

the pain of a divorce, or family cruelty, or the breakdown of relationships. Of course, all these things can be present in a Christian family, but there will always be the additional pain of spoken or unspoken opposition to the gospel and antagonism to God.

The teenage years can be a problem in a well-ordered Christian family. Even there the 'negotiations' involved in the de-parenting process can escalate into cosmic warfare at the breakfast table! But that process is further complicated in the non-Christian home when the young person is considering or has adopted a set of spiritual values opposed to those of the rest of the family. Here the youth leader will need wisdom and tact.

In these situations there is a sense in which a youth leader may find herself in the role of the parent. Job interceded with God continually for his sons in case they had sinned in their hearts (Job 1:5). Where the parents of a young person cannot pray for him and are indifferent to his spiritual welfare, the youth leader will have to take that burden on herself. Non-Christian parents cannot understand when their children become Christians and are not able to help them spiritually.

That does not always mean they don't want to, and that they would not like to share in the spiritual life their offspring have discovered—it may be God's purpose to bring the whole family to himself, starting with the younger generation—but, when they don't want to, the youth leader must continue to work within a firmly biblical frame of reference.

In other words, the fact that the young person is a Christian but the parents are not, does not overthrow the biblical order for the family. Children are not instructed to obey their parents only if their parents are Christians. While children, they are to obey Christian or non-Christian parents. Once adult, they are to respect and honour Christian or non-Christian parents.

In a sense, the gospel for the non-Christian parents of a Christian young person is largely that young person's obedience to them. If after his conversion the main difference his parents notice is that he never stops trying to evangelize them (implying in the process that what they brought him up to believe was not good enough for him), he may only end up alienating them. It is the youth worker's task to teach young people to obey their parents, before they start trying to evangelize them. If the parents notice a new and striking obedience in their child, then they are faced with a powerful testimony to the gospel which they will not be able to ignore.

So youth workers themselves will have to model respect for parents—not only for their own parents, but also for their young people's parents. They will want to respect the parents' wishes, even when those wishes are to curtail a young person's Christian activities.

For example, when a father says that he does not want his son to attend the youth group again until after his exams, the youth leader must show respect for that prohibition. The youth leader might visit the father and ask him to permit a limited attendance—perhaps on one day of the week with a promise that she will personally drive him home straight afterwards—but, if the father remains adamant the youth leader must come to terms with the fact that she is not the parent. That father will one day answer to God for the way he brought up his children, but it is unlikely that the long-term spiritual welfare of the son will be assisted by the youth leader encouraging direct disobedience to his parents.

Of course, there are situations where parents completely misuse their God-given authority. If a young person is forbidden to read the Bible or pray at home, then perhaps a different ethic will prevail, but such situations are rare. (I have only encountered one, when working with a young person from a Muslim family.)

Usually parents are motivated by a genuine (if sometimes misguided) concern for their child's welfare. The mature youth leader will accept that and seek to work with it rather than against it. She will always remember that the work of converting and nurturing the child is God's from beginning to end. It is God who has given us the command to obey our parents while we are children, and to respect them once we are adults. We can trust him to have got it right. The more we trust and seek to base our youth ministry on the Bible, the more he will be able to use us for his glory.

So there are dangers in the youth leader seeing herself as a substitute parent (although that may actually be true in some ways). Certainly we must take the home background of every young person seriously and be sensitive to the differences between a Christian family and a non-Christian family. We remember how Paul became 'all things to all men', so that he might by all means save some (1 Cor 9:22). He adapted himself to the Jew, who would have had a bellyful of religious instruction at home, and to the Gentile, who might well have had none (see 1 Cor 9:19-23).

The blackboard jungle

One area where adolescents spend a large part of their lives and where Christian youth work can be done is the school.

All young people in the UK today have to attend school up to the age of sixteen. At that age half the school population leaves, but youth unemployment is pressing larger numbers of young people to try tertiary education rather than the dole queue.

Because school is seen as essentially a part of the world of childhood, it is not an experience that is highly valued by young people in their aspiration for adulthood.

In general . . . most adolescents, whatever their attitude to study might be, found the constrictions and restraints and the lack of status this implied, irksome at best and extremely irritating at worst . . .

The common denominator was a propensity among the young to remonstrate against some of the restrictions imposed by the highly structured environments of school and against a lack of acknowledgement, by teachers, of the adolescents' changing status, i.e. their move away from childhood.[80]

A part-time job is often seen as more valuable for growing up because of the social experience it offers.[81] James Hemmings commented right back in 1962:

. . . adolescents have to attend to, and are largely absorbed by, certain inescapable tasks of development, such as learning to deal with a much increased capacity for feeling, establishing personal independence, mastering the arts of association and friendship, coming to terms with the other sex and personal sexuality, proving oneself through achievement, and working out a code of values by which to conduct personal life . . . secondary education pays little attention to these tasks of adolescent life so that the world of school and the inner world of adolescents tends to fall apart . . . adolescents get little educational assistance with their struggle to grow up as persons.[82]

For some, as we have already noted, school is a painful experience. Those in the lower academic bands 'often have to face a continuous set of implicit messages that they lack competence'.[83] Many will later regret that they did not do better at school, particularly as they search for employment. But all will look on their school days as part of the world of childhood and adolescence.

It will also be a place where young people experience the peer group in its most intense form. The pressure to conform on the young person at school can be enormous. The one who dares to be different invites scorn and isolation at a stage in his development when he is most vulnerable to what his peers think of him. It is the age when they tend to take messages about themselves more seriously from their peers than from adults. 'A teen will compromise his own identity in order to be accepted by his peers.'[84]

It is at school and college that the young Christian may find it hardest of all to live out his faith because of the overwhelming pressure to conform and his own fears of rejection by his peer group.

There are two immediate lessons to be drawn here for youth work. The first is that it will not be helpful to model the teaching programme of the youth fellowship on the classroom.

While it might appeal to the academically more able (the sort of person who is constantly affirmed by his academic success at school and who is bound for a university degree), it will alienate those of lower academic ability. More seriously, it will assert a cultural value which God himself denies (1 Cor 1:25-31). It will also tend to make Christianity look like part of the world of childhood, from which we naturally grow up.

Instead, it is important to teach the true value and purpose of education in the youth fellowship. Young people need to get their experience of academic education into a Christian perspective. The clever need to be taught not to despise the less clever. The assumption that education is just a means to an end (a better career or a larger wage packet) needs to be challenged. The whole notion of competition and self-improvement needs to be thought through with the help of the Holy Spirit. The teaching of Jesus (Mt 5:3-8) calls in question the basis of so many of our assumptions in this area.

It may be helpful to remind members of the youth group who are facing 'a continuous set of implicit messages that they lack competence' at school, that many others have struggled with their school work. Einstein was apparently told by one of his school teachers that he would never amount to anything. Charles Darwin did so badly at school that his father told him, 'You will be a disgrace to yourself and all your family.' The writer G.K. Chesterton was such a bad pupil that one of his teachers told him, 'If we could open your head we should not find any brain but only a lump of white fat.' School studies are a very limited measure of human ability.

Religious education is the one subject that must be taught in every school, and there is a special need in the youth fellowship to help those who are being taught about Christianity inaccurately. It is valuable to teach the young person to defend his or her Christian faith effectively in the classroom without arrogance or ill-manners.

It is also important that the whole ethos of the youth group is adult rather than childish and school-like. It must have a serious educational thrust to it, and it must be lively, but it must also be clear that what we are communicating is essential for adult life and is not just academic games. It is a call to maturity, and the atmosphere of the fellowship will benefit from reflecting that.

Positive thinking about peer pressure

The second lesson for youth ministry is that the young Christian who is spiritually isolated at school is very vulnerable.

James Dobson reports an interesting study in *Preparing for Adolescence*.[85] When nine members of a group of ten teenagers were instructed to vote for an obviously wrong answer, the tenth young person (who did not know the other nine had been instructed to vote wrongly) would almost always, after some hesitation, vote with the crowd against the clear evidence of his own eyes. However obvious the answer, if the nine voted wrongly, in 75% of the cases tested the tenth would vote along with them, rather than stand out against the crowd.

However, it was also discovered that if *just one other* teenager voted correctly, then the chances were greatly increased that number ten would also do what he thought was right. If just one other person will stand out against the group, then a young person gains courage to resist the pressure to conform.

In all too many schools there are young Christians walking around who never get to identify one another. They feel alone and isolated. They may never know that there was actually someone else in their class or year group who shared their convictions and was trying like them to march to the beat of a different drum.

If peer pressure can have a damaging effect on a young person's faith, it can also be beneficial. It is a matter of exposure to the right peer group. The pressure to conform to non-Christian standards can be counteracted by exposure to a Christian peer group. The peer group 'does not have to be a group of eighty kids; just one or two other teens who share his values is enough to give the teen encouragement and strength in handling the pressures'.[86]

Parents and youth leaders need to think positively about peer pressure and look for ways to use it on the side of the gospel. 'Of all the ties that hold young people to their faith, humanly speaking, the strongest by far is the association with other young people.'[87]

> Conformity to the peer group is the primary source of reassurance during early and mid-adolescence. Teenagers are very sensitive to the perceived differences between themselves and others. They will often judge themselves negatively on the basis of these differences.[88]

So a young Christian will need other young Christians alongside. They will support one another in their discipleship.

The CU

This is a strong argument for the existence of school and college Christian Unions. They provide a forum where Christian students can recognize one another. They show them that they are not alone. This is probably more important than the other functions of the Christian Union.

This function is sometimes called 'fellowship', but it is really 'identification', and the mutual encouragement that springs from that. By attending CU meetings the young person identifies himself as a Christian in the eyes of other Christians, and of non-Christians. This is in itself an act of witness to the school or college, and it is a gesture of solidarity with the faith of the other CU members. Regular attendance at CU meetings by an individual Christian can by itself make a powerful contribution to the spiritual lives of the other members.

'Fellowship' in the New Testament is something Christians have by doing things together. It may be prayer, it may be evangelism, it may be Christian teaching. All of these are valuable Christian activities for the CU.

In the absence of good youth fellowships in the local churches, a CU may have to have some of the functions that would normally belong to the local church, but this is never an ideal situation. As we saw in chapter seven, nothing can adequately replace the local community of faith in the life of the believer, whatever that believer's age.

On the other hand, the local church youth fellowships are often a very effective launching pad for school and college CUs. They can provide the back-up that helps to guide and support them. In fact, for many youth fellowships the local schools are the most natural spheres for evangelism.

It is here that many of their members spend a large number of their waking hours in close contact with non-Christians. So the youth leader must equip his young people to witness in their schools. For that they will need a living fellowship there in the shape of the CU. They will also need the opportunity provided by evangelistic events focused on the schools (but probably best organized by the churches).

Local church youth workers may be allowed to participate in RE lessons, either themselves or by bringing an outside team in for a specific period. Little will be achieved by deceit—cloaking 'hit and run' evangelism under a veneer of RE respectability—but much can be achieved by respecting the school authorities and co-operating with them to present Christianity to the pupils in an unemotional and academically respectable way.

Christian schoolteachers themselves will certainly need the support and encouragement of local churches. Close communication between youth leaders and the Christian teachers in local schools will be very valuable in evangelizing and discipling young people. When a school CU run by a teacher does not try (or is not able) to link up with the youth groups of local churches, both works are impoverished.

* * *

Understanding the educational system and the sort of pressures that face the young believer at school today is certainly important in youth ministry, but it is not as important as having a biblical understanding of the family—of how family life ought to work, of the pressures faced by the teenager at home, and of the differences between the young person from a Christian home and the young person from a non-Christian home.

We need to continue to bring the Bible's teaching to bear on both these areas of a young person's life. We will find that it will guide us step by step with the authentic voice of the living God.

9

Youth Today—Gone Tomorrow?
Strategies for church leadership

'It will only take you a couple of hours on a Sunday night,' says the minister after the morning service, as he tries to persuade someone to take on the youth leadership. 'Eight till ten . . . and perhaps half an hour for preparation some other time in the week. Just to provide something for the young people. It's a case of helping out until we can find someone to take over permanently. There's just no one else at the moment . . . .'

The prospective leader is not at all clear what he is being offered. He has a shrewd suspicion that the minister is lying, because he usually is when he says anything will only take 'a couple of hours'. The prospective leader also has a vague sense that it is probably a life sentence, because he's heard the one about 'someone taking over permanently' before too. But the knockout punch comes in the last line—'there's no one else to do it'—and all the guilt that implies if he refuses to catch the ball before it falls to the ground.

So another person takes on youth work, hoping to squeeze it into a few minutes of his already over-full schedule, and longing to be relieved of the burden at the earliest opportunity. It is a recipe for disaster and no one—not the young people, nor the minister, nor the rest of the church, nor the youth leader himself—is going to benefit from it.

I hope it will have become clear by now that Christian youth work is not something that can be done effectively by someone who is already busy with other things. It cannot be an added extra in local church life, tacked on because the church leader cannot bear the thought of his church not having any youth work. If it is worth doing at all, it is worth doing properly. If it is going to be done properly, it is going to require the right people, with the time and the energy to do it.

People not programmes

God equips his people with what they need to function as he means them to (Eph 4:7-16). Both as individuals and as the church, he intends us only to tackle the tasks that we are capable of doing well for him, but sometimes we take on more tasks than he has equipped us for. This is particularly true of the local church where the church leader over-extends the ministry beyond the resources available.

Instead of doing a few things excellently for God, we end up doing a great many things badly. We are unable to pursue excellence because we are pursuing far too many things. The life of the local church can actually be impoverished rather than enriched by the width of the activities in which it is engaged. If they are all done poorly because the Christians are so overstretched, little glory will come to God. 'Do less, better' is a slogan that some of us (and some of our churches) might profitably adopt.

Youth work is no exception. There will be times when it is better not to start youth work in a particular church. It is not a case of 'anything is better than nothing'.

I am not saying that no youth work should be started until the perfect youth leader appears. In fact the notion of the ideal youth leader—young, good-looking, witty, contemporary, fashionable, with a degree in theology and authentic street credibility—is not helpful. Youth work is about people and not about programmes or structures. God's answer to his people's problems is usually a man rather than a plan. He raises up people to do his work, often people who are humanly speaking quite unpromising: 'For consider your call, brethren; not many of you were wise according to worldly standards, not many were powerful, not many were of noble birth' (1 Cor 1:26). But they are people with a concern to serve him and to do his will as best they can.

The quality of the youth work in a local church will always be related to the spiritual quality of the people leading the work. However good the resources and structures, however sound the strategy, it is the youth leaders themselves who are the key.

I have already argued (in chapter seven) that the responsibility for youth work lies with the local church. It is the local church leadership who are responsible for the young people of their fellowship and of the area, just as much as they are responsible for the adults. It is they who should expect God to guide them directly about youth work and to equip their congregations for it. (They cannot pass that responsibility on to a national youth organization or a denominational youth structure, although they may well receive help, advice, resources and training from those sources.)

So we will consider how the leadership of the local church can discharge those obligations. As the key to youth work is people, it is the task of the church leadership to enable the right people to do the right job in the right way. Many church leaders lament that they just do not have anyone to start youth work, but it might be helpful for them to think about what they would offer that person from their side.

A five-point strategy for youth work

1. Commitment and prayer

The first thing a youth worker needs to receive from the church leadership is a strong sense that the church leaders are as committed to the task as he is. In appointing a youth leader, the minister is not passing the buck for youth work. Responsibility may be delegated, but it is not abrogated. He is not washing his hands of the matter and hoping he will hear no more about the young people for many years to come.

The 'it's-all-over-to-you-now' attitude does not reflect the shared ministry of the New Testament. Jesus sent out the seventy disciples two by two (Lk 10:1). Paul was constantly teaming up with people and seems to have been far from happy when he found himself alone (2 Tim 4:9-18). Youth work is particularly demanding in time and energy, and it drains the emotions of those involved. Youth leaders must know that the rest of the church leadership is committed to what they are doing, is interested in how the work is developing, and is available to give support, advice and encouragement.

Practically, this will entail a regular system for reporting back, and structured prayer support. If the youth leader is working in a particularly exposed situation—where there is little or no Christian nucleus to start from, where the young people come from disadvantaged backgrounds alienated from the church, or where he is expected to break into new territory—he will need a special support group whose task is to monitor and pray for his activities. The members of that group should be selected by the church leaders and the youth worker together. It is important that he does not feel isolated.

The ideal will be to form a team of youth leaders. It is not always possible at first, but the Bible would suggest that God does not mean us to be alone in ministry. Husband and wife teams can be effective, but a team that includes the married and the unmarried will have greater wisdom, greater flexibility and a greater ability to relate to different young people. It will need to include both sexes.

To speak of a team of youth leaders may be hopelessly idealistic in terms of the realities of much local church life, but if the ideal is valid, the question is: how does the church leadership take one small step in that direction? The answer is: by its own commitment to, and prayer for, young people's work.

Many ministers think they will give serious attention to the needs of young people when somebody suitable to be a youth leader turns up, but if they started to pray for and be concerned about young people, they might be surprised at how quickly a suitable youth leader appears. God guides his people as they walk, one step at a time. The first step is commitment and prayer. This step comes before starting any actual youth work.

2. Vision and planning

It is the task of the church leadership to have a vision for the whole church. It is also their task to communicate that vision to each part of the church, and to let each part of the church know how it fits into the overall vision. The Authorized Version translation of Proverbs 29:18 reads: 'Where there is no vision, the people perish.' For the sake of the people, the church leadership must ask God to give them a clear vision of what he wants to happen in that congregation. Then they will need his help to share that vision with his people.

Paul seems to have had plans and a strategy (subject to the Lord's overruling)[89] on his missionary journeys (see Acts 19:21; Rom 15:22-25). Like Jesus (Mk 1:35-39; Lk 5:15-16), his ministry was proactive rather than reactive.

In practical terms, having a vision means having a plan—or rather, planning. Planning is the first stage in turning a vision into reality. It casts a net over the future. The more energy and prayer that goes into planning, the greater the likelihood that the vision will come about.

Planning must be visionary. It must be proactive rather than reactive. Instead of looking at what is and asking how to maintain it, it should look at what ought to be and ask how to bring it about. Ted Kennedy, in his funeral oration for his brother, said, 'Some men see things as they are and say "why?" But

Bobby dreamed things that never were, and said, "Why not?" That is the task for church leadership.

In the situation of the youth and children's work of the local church, there may be a big gap between how things are and how they ought to be. There may be nothing happening at all, in which case the church leadership must resist the temptation to let sleeping dogs lie. Or there may be a flourishing work at some age levels, but nothing at others.

A common pattern is a fairly large Sunday School for the up-to-twelve-year-olds, and then a rapid decline (or even a complete vacuum) thereafter. The temptation here is to continue to reinforce the success of the Sunday School, while neglecting the youth fellowship. There may be an able Sunday School co-ordinator who could be given oversight of the youth work as well. There may be someone teaching a Sunday School class well, who could be moved up to work with the teenagers. It may be right to inform the whole congregation of the area where the leadership believes there needs to be growth and development, and to focus their prayers on it for a year.

The youth leader himself will need a vision for his work, and his vision must relate to the vision of the church leadership for the whole church. To some extent it is the task of the church leadership to provide the youth leader with his vision. He will always work better if he sees how his work fits into the whole picture and if he feels part of a larger purpose. It will encourage him to plan for his own ministry.

If there is no planning in the rest of the church, the youth leader will not be encouraged to plan or to have specific targets and goals for the young people. Without planning, there will be no practical expression of vision. The youth work will meander aimlessly and any life will go out of it.

3. Management

The most time-consuming aspect of the church leadership's obligations to the youth work is management. It consists of at least three things.

(a) A clear job description. Instead of the vague offer with
which this chapter began, no one should be asked to take on a
task in the local church without being provided with the clear-
est possible picture of what will be involved. Unless a prospective youth leader has a clear idea of what youth leadership is,
he is unlikely to fulfil the role to his or anyone else's satisfaction. If the church leadership is not yet clear what is involved, then there must be a proper discussion with the youth
leader until both sides agree a job description.[90]

A key element is the number of hours per week that will be
involved. Few people are in a position to make an open-ended
commitment of their time. Without appropriate boundaries
being drawn from the outset, there will be a continual element
of guilt, which will damage the leader spiritually. He will
always feel that he has not done enough and that he ought to
be doing more. It is the job of the church leadership to protect
their people from those feelings of guilt.

The leader needs to know what he is expected to do, when
he has fulfilled those obligations, and where he should draw
the boundaries, so that he does not become overcommitted
and lose the balance of his own life. Because youth work
involves opening up our lives to young people in order that
they may learn the comprehensive nature of the Christian
faith from us, such boundaries are especially important.

It may be difficult to convey this picture in words alone.
Where there is already youth work happening in a fellowship
(or in a neighbouring fellowship), the prospective leader can
first approach it as a spectator. The church leadership might
suggest that he joins the present youth leader(s) for a period,
just as an observer. Once he has had a close look at what is
involved, then there can be a proper discussion about making
a commitment to it.

If there is no youth work at present, and the future leader
has had no previous experience, it is all the more important
for him to get a close look at youth work in action. A training

weekend or course is better than nothing. A Christian camp or houseparty will be better still. Best of all, however, will be a situation as similar to his own as possible, where he can watch and reflect and discuss, before plunging in. There are many people struggling to do youth work in the local church, who have never had the opportunity to watch other people doing youth work. Where the circumstances are very discouraging (small numbers, little response), vision is hard for the youth leader who has never seen anything else.

So the prospective leader must know what is being taken on, and there must be agreement with the church leadership about what the job requires.

(b) A contract. It may sound grand and idealistic to speak of a 'contract', but proper management involves people knowing how long they are expected to shoulder a particular responsibility. Without agreement on this, guilt will raise its ugly head again. People continue in particular tasks long after they should have resigned, because they feel they will be 'letting the vicar down' if they give up.

There is a correct, God-given imperative that keeps us in Christian ministry: 'Woe to me if I do not preach the gospel!' (1 Cor 9:16), but specific responsibilities within the life of the local church benefit from regular review. They do not benefit from heavy agendas of guilt carried by people who feel stuck because they know the church leaders will be disconcerted if they try to resign.[91]

So it is helpful to have an informal agreement about how long a youth leader is to do the job. Just as there needs to be an induction period during which the leader can form a clear picture of the task, there also needs to be a probationary period before a firm commitment is made. The 'contract' might be for a three-month probationary period first. During that time the leader gets some first-hand experience of youth leading, and, at the end of it, he may decide that he does not want any more. Or the church leadership may decide he is not suited to it. Perhaps they can see it is damaging his marriage and his family, or some fact emerges about his past which they had not known before and which makes it unwise to have him working with young people, or the other leaders cannot work with him, or it is clear that his understanding of the job is incompatible with their expectations.

Whatever the circumstances, it is understood that at the end of the probation the arrangement can be ended by either party after discussion. This has several advantages. It allows the nervous leader to have a gentle introduction to youth work, without having to make a serious, long-term commitment. There are many youth leaders who would never have started at all if they had not been allowed to start gently, so that their early misgivings were gradually overcome by actual contact with young people. It also provides an extended period during which both sides can try to discern God's will accurately in the matter. It cannot be a snap decision on the spot. It has to be thought about, prayed over and discussed.

If both parties agree at the end of the three months, then the informal contract might be extended for one year, or two years. It is wise to keep it fairly short. The mobility of modern society increases each year and, however much the leadership may long for a degree of permanence in the organizational structures of the local church, they are unlikely to achieve it.

A short contract may actually prove a more serious commitment than a longer one. If a leader undertakes to lead the youth work for a year, after serious thought and prayer, then he is more likely to think twice when he is offered promotion in his work that entails a move across the country two months after he starts. If God guided him to take on youth leadership, then God is probably not behind the new career opportunity. Christians who turn down promotion at work for the sake of their Christian ministry are a powerful testimony in our society.

It is also good for the church leadership to be forced to review the youth leaders regularly by the termination of their contracts. 'Fire-fighting' management, which intervenes only if a crisis arises, is a poor model for Christian work. The local church needs 'hands-on' management, where the overall leadership exercises a continuous concern for the work. This need not be an interfering concern—it can be very light and trusting—but the youth leader knows that he is not forgotten about. He also knows that he can step out of the work without any acrimony or guilt at a specified date.

(c) Accountability. The third element in management is that the individual should know to whom he is accountable, and should expect to be assessed.[92]

How many people in local church life have never been told whether they are doing their jobs well or badly? Most people soldier on, not particularly clear what their actual job is, and certainly unaware of whether they are doing it well or whether they could be doing it better. We all need assessment. Without it we do not achieve our potential.

It is important that this is agreed upon at the beginning, however. Once someone has been doing a job in the local church for a year or two, it is very hard then to start assessing her. A new initiative to increase accountability will inevitably be interpreted as a threat—she will think she can't have been doing the job properly, otherwise the rules wouldn't be changing now.

Not only must assessment be agreed from the outset, it must also consist primarily of encouragement. It is said that we need to be praised five times as often as we are criticized. Unless the assessment consists mainly of encouragement, any criticism offered will never be taken constructively. It will be seen as a threat, and it will be handled defensively by the recipient. But, if the main content of assessment is praise, affirmation and encouragement (this must not be false—we can make people feel good about what they are doing without necessarily telling them that they are doing it well), then we will have built a firm bridge for constructive criticism. They will be able to hear what we say without being threatened, and they will be able to improve their work in the light of what we say.

So someone must be assessing the youth leader—not in order to criticize her, but so that she is encouraged, so that she feels a part of the whole church, and so that she is able to become a better youth leader. This does not have to be the vicar or pastor himself. There may be a church warden or a member of the PCC or an elder in the congregation who will watch over the youth and children's work. But the individual youth leader must know from the start that she will be meeting someone briefly from time to time to chat over her work with the young people.

If the arrangement is too haphazard, it will not fulfil its purpose because the leader will not have that vital sense of belonging to a team. If no arrangement is made, then 'firefighting' management takes over. The first time anyone says anything to the youth leader about the youth work is when something has gone wrong. Interference at this point is unlikely to be appreciated, however, when no one stood beside her and encouraged her when things were going well. It will probably cause bitterness and resentment.

Within a team of youth leaders the senior one can assess his colleagues, but he himself must be accountable to the church leadership. In experience, this is the link that is most likely to be missing. It should have been built in by the church leadership from the start. It is always worth having, and many of the problems of youth work in the local church are caused by its absence.

4. Training

Training is an aspect of management, but it is important enough to be considered separately.[93]

This is the responsibility of the church leadership. We cannot expect youth leaders to take the initiative and get themselves trained. Many do, but the church leadership should have made it clear right away that training was necessary and that they wanted it to happen. The church leadership is not required to provide the training, because it may not be able to, but it is the responsibility of the church leadership to see that it happens.

All too often people get their first training after they have been doing a task in the local church for some time, and they probably have to pay for it themselves. Some churches and fellowships may not be in a position to fund the training of their leaders, but most can at least subsidize it, and many can pay in full, particularly where there is a fund for the youth and children's work. The fact that many youth leaders are prepared to pay for their own training (and are better informed on where to look for it) should not deter the church leadership from taking the initiative in instigating training, and ensuring that it happens.

Training may well be on the job and from within the local team. The principle of accountability will encourage this. The most effective training takes place when an inexperienced leader works alongside an experienced leader, when they watch each other in action and reflect together on what they are doing and how they might do it better.

However, the opportunity to go on a course or to attend a residential training conference will also be beneficial. The church leadership should encourage them to find a suitable one and, if possible, should offer to pay for it and for any travel expenses. An offer to subsidize the cost may be sufficient encouragement (if the fellowship really is unable to fund it fully).

Training is a part of the initiation for youth leadership. It should not be necessary to say that it must come at the beginning rather than at the end! This is particularly important where youth work is being started for the first time, and so there is no possibility of on-the-job training. To start up local church youth work without any experience and without the prospect of any training is a hard task indeed. It would be better for the prospective youth leader to join the leadership team of another church's youth work for a time (even if it means a regular drive of some distance and a delay in starting the new youth work), or waiting to attend a suitable course or training conference first.

God equips us for ministry as we serve him. The leadership of the local congregation can expect to see that happen as their youth leaders improve with training and experience. They should build that expectation into their church life and plan to be the Holy Spirit's instrument in constantly raising the standard of the youth leaders.

5. Resources

The final thing a youth leader can expect to receive from his church leadership is the resources necessary to do the work. As God, in calling us to his service, assures that he will supply all we need to serve and obey him (Phil 4:19), so the youth worker needs to know how his needs will be met.

There may be situations where she has to be told that there are no funds available for youth work, and any money she wants to spend she will have to raise herself. That will be sad, but at least she must be told it clearly, so that she knows where she stands.

Effective youth work will cost money. It will be needed for equipment, teaching materials, subscriptions and affiliation fees to national organizations, and leaders' training. Most significantly, it will be needed to subsidize activities for the young people.

Without money for this, the activity programme will favour those members who have the money to pay for trips, outings, camps and houseparties, and it will exclude those who do not. The alternative is for the youth leader to curtail the activity programme until it is within the reach of all the members' pockets, but it is far better to have the resources available to do ambitious things without favouring the wealthy and excluding the poor.[94] If the church will not subsidize the young people's activities, then the youth leader should set up a fund to even out the differences between the young people's backgrounds. This is a practical way of making sure the youth work has no bias towards the privileged.

It is to be hoped that most fellowships will budget to pay for their youth work. The church budget can be a valuable planning instrument. It can be one way that the church leadership express their vision for the future of the congregation, and one way they put their priorities into practice. In fact, the first practical step towards starting youth work in a church might be for the church leadership to put a figure into the budget for youth work, even though no youth work exists as yet.

Some church councils generously offer to underwrite the youth and children's work of the church. 'Just tell us what you spend,' they say to the youth leaders, 'and we'll give you a cheque.' That may be generous, but it is not the best way of operating. By budgeting specifically, they can give the youth work the priority they think it should have in the church's spending. They will also be encouraging the youth leaders to plan how best to use the resources available. They may even want to suggest how the youth leaders spend the money: so much on training, so much on subsidizing youth activities, etc. They will certainly want a report on how it has been spent at the end of the year.

Other churches refuse to accept any financial responsibility for youth work. Such fellowships are rare (and their leaders are unlikely to be reading this book!), but where a youth leader encounters this situation, there are still plans he can implement. The most common is fund-raising events by the young people themselves, where the money raised is divided between a charity and funding the youth work.

Some youth leaders redirect the proportion of their own giving that would go to their home church into the youth work, until the church takes responsibility for that work itself. This is done with the full knowledge of the church leadership and the church treasurer. In fact, it is useful to ask the treasurer himself to administer a separate youth fund, so that the whole fellowship can know exactly what is going on and other members (particularly the parents of the young people) can contribute to the fund as well, if they want to.

It is surprising how much money can be mobilized for youth work in this way (when Christians allocate part of their giving to some Christian work in which they are directly involved themselves, they often find themselves giving more generously than they normally would). It is also surprising how quickly the church leadership may prefer to budget properly for the youth work in future. It will prove a wise investment.

Great ideals, but grim realities

As you have read this five-point strategy, you may have felt that it is written for a situation a million miles away from where your local church is at the moment. I am sorry if it has sounded hopelessly idealistic, but we do need an idea of how things *should* work, even if that ideal is a long way away at present. We also need to be clear about the first steps we can take towards that distant ideal. 'The journey of a thousand miles begins with a single step.'

So many church leaders lament that their church cannot do youth work because they have no one to do it, but they overlook what they could already be doing to express their commitment to young people, in anticipation of God providing them with suitable youth leadership. To pray for youth work and to budget for it are the first steps to realizing their vision. Until they take them, God may not do his part in answering their prayer for a leader.

This five-point strategy applies to every sort of Christian youth work. Whether the model in the church leadership's mind is of a 'closed' nurture group type or a more 'open' youth club variety, their responsibilities towards it are the same. If they do not fulfil them, they will be weakening the youth work and increasing the probability of it being a problem area in the church's life.

I have already argued that the distinction between 'open'

and 'closed' youth work is unhelpful and theologically uncertain (see chapters five, six and seven). There are biblical patterns for communicating the faith (whether in evangelism or in nurture) that should be normative for every area of the local church's life, but starting youth work in the local church may mean choosing an appropriate point on the open/closed spectrum at which to begin.

There may already be a group of spiritually-hungry young people at hand, or there may be no evidence of any spiritual hunger whatsoever among young people in the area. In the light of their particular circumstances, each fellowship has to create its own custom-built structure for youth ministry. In every case, however, they will be trying to discover what God is already doing and to relate their plans to his purposes. They must take seriously the Bible's guidance on how youth work should be done, and they must check their church's practices against the scriptural principles I have tried to outline in this book.

There are certain recurrent problem areas in Christian youth work and, having spent some time looking at an ideal 'model' in this chapter so far, we will now get our feet firmly back on the ground by considering the most common of them.

1. The life of the leader

There are the problems which relate to the personal life of the leader. I suggested in chapter eight that God has set an order of priority in every individual's relationships.

First the church leadership must be satisfied that the youth leader has established and is maintaining his own relationship with God. Congregations are often careful to check that the youth leader is converted, but they may not be watching so carefully to see whether he is continuing to grow spiritually. His leadership of the young people must not be allowed to damage his own spiritual life and growth. This is not always easy to discern, but wise church leaders will have it in their thoughts and prayers. For example, is their church life structured in such a way that the youth and children's leaders rarely get to hear a sermon?

Then the youth leader's relationship with his own family must not be jeopardized by the youth work. After marriage, the Israelite was excused from military service for a year. 'When a man is newly married, he shall not go out with the army or be charged with any business; he shall be free at home one year, to be happy with his wife whom he has taken' (Deut 24:5). So the very recently married should take time off youth leadership. The first few months of marriage are so vital for laying the foundations of a life-long relationship that they must not be interfered with by the intrusion of young people into the emotional life of the couple (and no one can do Christian youth work without young people intruding into his or her emotional life).

It is better to delay the start of youth work for twelve months and allow the couple to lay the basis for a life-long Christian marriage. However keen they may be to get back into 'shared ministry', the wise church leader will point the eager young couple back to God's priorities. He will not put the needs of his church before their need to build a stable marriage. (The wise leader of Christian camps and house-parties will exercise the same self-restraint and tell members of his team to take a year off when they get married.)

There is a need for Christians involved in youth work who are modelling a stable and God-centred marriage to young people. It is hard for young people from broken homes to grow up to build stable families themselves, unless they have been able to see a secure marriage at close quarters. For this reason, youth ministry may not be the right area of Christian service for a divorced person. Church leaders may want to think hard before asking a divorced person to take on this particular task. There may be other areas of the fellowship's life where that person might be better able to use his or her gifts and abilities. It is the responsibility of church leaders to try to ensure that their young people have a helpful model of

Christian marriage presented to them.

The third level of relationships where trouble can easily arise is when the youth leader's loyalty to the youth group exceeds his loyalty to the church leadership. Loyalty begets loyalty, and the youth leader must know that the church leaders will not criticize him behind his back. For example, he must know that the youth work will not be reviewed by the church's governing body in his absence.

The church leadership cannot guarantee the loyalty of the youth leader, but they can go a long way to encourage it—by their own loyalty to him, by their obvious commitment to the work he is doing, and by making it clear from the start that they will expect him to be loyal to them. If he presents the young people with a model of disloyalty to the rest of the church, he is doing great spiritual damage.

2. Adult church versus youth group: the great divide

This leads to another common trouble spot in local church youth work—the problem of a young people's work that is not integrated into the life of the adult church, and, in some cases, appears to have no relationship to it at all.

As I have already suggested in the preceeding paragraphs, the solution to this problem lies primarily in the life of the youth leader herself. If she is a deeply committed, regularly worshipping member of the adult congregation, her own life will be the most powerful bridge between the young people and the adult church. Like all good bridges, this one needs to be well secured at both ends. Her love for the young people and her love for the church will inevitably fuse and communicate both ways. As the young people respect and love her, they will catch her love for the church.

So, if the church leadership finds that there is a great chasm opening up between the young people and the rest of the church, their first port of call is the youth leader. They may need to go further back in their relationship with her and make sure that they are providing her with all the things she can reasonably expect of them (as listed in the five-point strategy for youth work).

If they are, then they should be in a position to discuss with her (and the rest of the youth leadership team, if there is one) what can be done to bridge the chasm. First of all there must be good biblical teaching about the nature of the church and what it means to belong to it (see chapter seven).

There must also be a balance between all-age activities in the church and peer-group activities. It might be necessary to curtail the youth group programme to allow the young people time and energy to participate in the life of the rest of the church. It might be necessary to make the older church activities and the main services more attractive to the young.

There are various ways that personal contact can be increased between the old and the young, but this rarely works with groups. You may be able to get the youth group en masse to attend a service which they don't normally come to, but they will probably stick together as a group. The rest of the congregation may even find their group presence unsettling and rather threatening. Similarly there may be a value in getting them to lead a service in the church, but it does not usually achieve the purpose of getting the old and the young to meet one another. In fact, it can encourage the adults to regard the young people as liturgical sea-lions, brought out of their cages every so often to perform for the adults in a youth service!

It is much better to work on an individual level. Individual adults can (and should) be systematically involved in the youth group programme—as speakers, guest celebrities to be interviewed, members of brains trusts, helpers with transport or hospitality, etc. Some churches run adoption schemes where members of the youth group are adopted by older members of the congregation for prayer and hospitality; or some of the oldest members of the congregation are adopted by members of the youth group for visiting and practical help. Individual members of the youth group can be invited to help conduct the ordinary services of the church. If this is done regularly and systematically, it may prove more helpful than occasional youth services (which can be traumatic events that only underline the gap between the old and the young).

The way the young meet the old most effectively is when one young person and one old person get to know and love each other. Every avenue must be explored to enable that to happen. It will happen at the level of individuals. Rarely does it happen at the level of groups.

Above all, there must be a commitment on both sides—by the adult leadership and by the youth leadership—to the unity of the body of Christ. The Bible does not encourage me to think that we will ever finally resolve the tensions between the old and the young in this present age (see pages 164–165). These tensions will continue to appear in the life of the church, but there should be a continuous and powerful resolve on the part of the leadership not to allow them to damage the spiritual life of the congregation. It is this mutual, biblical commitment which is the fundamental solution to the problem, whatever particular strategies different church situations may require.

3. The very small group

A third problem area is the question of very low numbers. The study of group dynamics suggests that once a group reaches a certain size, it will build up its own momentum and be attractive to outsiders, but below a certain number, the group will have a tendency to lose members and to dwindle away.

This may be a valid observation of how groups usually work, and some of the findings of group dynamics may be reflected in the New Testament, but there are no biblical grounds for valuing a large youth group above a small one. It is our culture which tells us that 'big is beautiful'. The Bible suggests God reverses that value: 'It was not because you were more in number than any other people that the Lord set his love upon you and chose you, for you were the fewest of all peoples' (Deut 7:7).

Church leaders need to guard their youth leaders against unhelpful pressures to get results in their youth work. It may be the pressure of the expectations of the rest of the congregation, or it may be the pressure of a results-orientated (rather than obedience-orientated) theology. There is a right and helpful pressure that comes from a vision of God's desire to reach young people. It is his purpose that the gospel should multiply throughout the world. It is right to have ambitious goals when they are given by him, because he will then also supply the energy to reach them (Col 1:29).

There are, however, also pressures that merely induce guilt in the youth leader. No youth leader ever did his work better for carrying a load of unnecessary guilt on his shoulders. There are situations, particularly in rural areas, where the scope for the youth work to grow is strictly limited. There are other situations where the youth work may have to get smaller (sometimes drastically so) before it can grow again. This will be the case where a youth work has grown up that is not based on biblical foundations.

Often in the life of a youth group there are growth spurts followed by periods of consolidation, when numbers may even fall slightly. Growth in the life of a youth group is not always numerical—there may be relational growth between the members, or growth in their knowledge of biblical truth, or growth in their desire to serve God in the world (although these will usually lead on to numerical growth, where the opportunity for it exists).

The youth leader must know that the church leadership's support for him does not depend on his producing certain results in the youth work. He must be freed from that sort of pressure.

On the other hand, the church leadership can use the insights of group dynamics and try to create the circumstances that are most favourable to growth. Where a small group of

Christian young people have a sense of isolation, it will be encouraging to link them up with other Christian teenagers. This may have to be in the form of occasional events like houseparties, camps, rallies, or national weekends.

It may be possible to arrange some more permanent co-operation between local churches in order to create a group of young people of a viable size. Some areas have regular celebration events for young people where several youth groups come together and encourage one another. In isolated situations, money is never wasted when it is spent on transport to bring young Christians into contact with one another.

Theoretically, it is possible for several churches which have no youth work to pool their resources in order to get some started. In practice, once the youth group begins to develop its own life, there is a natural tendency for all the young people to want to attend the same church. Then the other churches feel that they have lost their young people to the chosen church. This would seem to be a much better situation than no youth work at all, but not all church leaders have the magnanimity to accept the loss of their few remaining teenagers to another church!

The small group need not be a problem where it is not seen as a problem by the leaders. It can actually represent an opportunity—an opportunity to disciple young people in more depth than is possible in a larger group. We need to remember again the way Jesus focused his ministry. It is sad to hear of a church which has closed its youth work because 'there were only a handful of young people left'. How grateful we all are that the Son of God did not cancel his mission to earth when he only had twelve disciples and one of them a traitor!

4. The boy/girl balance

A further common problem in youth work is the fact that we frequently attract more girls than boys to the youth programme.

This may seem to be a problem for the youth leadership

rather than the church leadership, but it is usually a wider problem than just the youth work. Often there is a considerable imbalance in the sexes throughout the congregation. The problem may have its roots in the youngest Sunday School classes, where the model of grown-up Christianity which we present to the children is usually feminine. The absence of adult Christian males working lower down the age range may help to explain why more boys than girls drop out of the church's youth work at puberty. Church leaders should bear this in mind when they appoint Sunday School teachers.

Youth leaders are not always sensitive to some of the developmental differences between girls and boys during adolescence. Girls mature earlier and many youth group programmes are unconsciously designed to suit their needs rather than those of their male peers. The girls are better at handling discussions and have greater social skills. Simmons and Wade in the concluding chapter of their book underline this distinction:

> Girls, more than boys, tend to hold beliefs that are less materialistic and more to do with interpersonal relationships. Whether this is to do with some natural endowment or whether it is a function of the attitudes of the society in which we live is difficult to say, but whatever the cause it is one of the most consistent findings in this survey.[95]

John Nicholson also points out that adolescence is the 'period of life when we are most conservative about sex roles'.[96]

Sitting around a room, studying the Bible and singing choruses are not activities well suited to the fourteen-year-old boy, who may be self-conscious of his recently broken voice and not at all at ease in mixed company. But his female contemporary may find them quite congenial. It may be necessary to correct this bias in the youth programme by deliberately adding certain physical activities for the boys. It is interesting to note that in secular open youth work there is an imbalance in the opposite direction, with more boys than girls. Many youth leaders keep a close eye on the sex balance in their groups, because they know how hard it is to attract boys into a group once it has become dominated by girls.

This is another area where the church leadership needs to be aware of the problem and strongly supportive of the youth leaders, particularly if other members of the congregation are critical of the measures taken to maintain a balance.

*   *   *

All too often the youth work of the local church is weak and the church leaders feel guilty about it. I have not intended to increase that feeling of guilt in this chapter. I hope I have provided some ideas for practical first steps in establishing youth work. I hope I have also provided some guidelines for maintaining good communications and a warm and supportive relationship with the youth leaders—because that is the key that unlocks so many youth work problems.[97]

10

Where the Rubber Meets the Road
A finale for youth leaders

Resource points

In writing this book, my intention was not to produce a practical handbook for youth workers. I aimed to provide a theoretical and biblical treatment of youth work as a theological foundation for the youth ministry of the local church. However, I am aware that there may be readers who are crying out for practical help, and they may find it in the index of resource agencies at the back (page 249). Inevitably that index will date quickly; addresses change and new organizations appear. It is also a personal list. I have not attempted a comprehensive survey. I am only providing the names of organizations with which I have some experience.

Not all of them would approach youth work along the lines I have suggested in this book. The reader can decide for himself how true their approach is to the Bible and how appropriate their resources are to his particular situation.

Nationally-produced materials should always be scrutinized carefully by the local youth leader. However good the resources provided by a national organization, they are always improved when the leader adapts them for his own local situation. God has appointed him to feed those particular sheep. In making us under-shepherds, God also equips us for the task. He will provide us with the judgement to know what is right for our young people and the ability to adapt material to meet their needs. We can be confident that no one knows better than we what our sheep need.

So we can have the confidence to leave things out, abbreviate sections, insert material from other sources, and provide our own explanations and illustrations. We should not leave our critical faculties on one side just because some course material comes from a well-known Christian organization.

Some resources provided for local church youth work are excellent in terms of communication. They are right on the teenager's wavelength, with good educational techniques, and a lively, humorous, attention-grabbing approach. But what they actually communicate may not be biblical at all. It may have only very slim links with Christian doctrine, if any.

On the other hand, there is other material with excellent content but terrible presentation. The youth leader has to work overtime to bring it to life and to relate it to the real world of his young people.

The danger is that the first of these two types of material is the easier to use. We are all grateful for having something which our young people will enjoy and which will save us time in preparation, but if it does not teach the truths that save and sanctify men and women, then it will have no eternal value. It is going to cost us time and mental energy to prepare palatable spiritual food for our young people, but it is a responsibility we must not shirk. (What God thinks of shepherds who do not feed his sheep is spelt out very clearly in Ezekiel 34.)

It is important not to over-rate the attention span of a young people's group. Careful preparation is the key to bringing pace, variety and liveliness into a teaching session.There are a number of techniques for maintaining interest: the size of the group can be frequently changed (sometimes in pairs, or sub-groups of four, then all together again); a speaker can be interrupted after ten minutes and the group divided up into buzz-groups for a couple of minutes to come back with one question on what he has said so far; the youth leader can add a bit of personal testimony in the middle of course material; a film or video can be stopped before the end and the group asked to discuss how they think it will end.[98]

I hope that the youth leader searching for practical help will find it from the sources I have listed. This book has indicated a biblical framework for youth ministry, and has sought to provide help in assessing the value of those sources. But there are many aspects of the work that I have not been able to cover.

Youth work touches on every aspect of Christian teaching and every area of church life. Much of what I have written applies with equal force to the adult life of the church. The strategies for church leadership in chapter nine, for example, are equally applicable to any leadership tasks within a fellowship.

Basic teaching

I would like to have provided an outline of the main Christian doctrines that have particular relevance in youth work, but all Christian teaching has some bearing on youth work, and to attempt a systematic theology would be beyond my powers and beyond the reader's patience.

It is worth saying, however, that Christian youth leaders need to develop their understanding of certain doctrines in particular. I have already considered the centrality of the cross and the importance of a thoroughly biblical understanding of conversion. The youth worker will find it valuable to be able to explain very simply and biblically how someone can respond to the gospel. Young people are at a key stage for decision-making. They have the energy and mental flexibility and humility to consider tough issues and to change their minds about them.

There are a number of simple gospel outlines that can be learnt by heart. It will be useful for the youth worker to have one at her fingertips. Opportunities to explain how to become a Christian simply and briefly are too important to miss. Although I had been involved in the outward trappings of religion for nearly two decades, it was not until someone explained to me three simple steps I needed to take that I became a Christian.

He told me first that I had to *admit* I was not a Christian already and that my sin had cut me off from God. He showed me Romans 3:23—'All have sinned and fall short of the glory of God'—and I saw the universal extent of sin. Then he showed me Romans 6:23—'The wages of sin is death'—and I saw the inescapable consequence of my sin: separation from God and eternal death. In my heart of hearts I already knew that I did not have a real relationship with God, but now I understood why I was separated from him.

Then he told me that I had to *believe* that Jesus died on the cross to take the consequence of my sin. He showed me Isaiah 53:6—'All we like sheep have gone astray; we have turned every one to his own way; and the Lord has laid on him the iniquity of us all'—and he explained that it was a prophecy about Jesus Christ. For the first time I realized that God had punished Jesus Christ for my sin, and he could forgive me because someone else had died in my place. Jesus had been separated from God so that I need not be.

Thirdly, my friend told me that I had to *come* to God and to accept his free forgiveness. He showed me Revelation 3:20 and told me that they could be the words of Jesus knocking at my heart: 'Behold, I stand at the door and knock; if any one hears my voice and opens the door, I will come in to him and eat with him, and he with me.' I realized that through his Holy Spirit Jesus could come into my life there and then, to take command of what was rightfully his.

So I did. I continue to have a great faith in that simple gospel outline:

1. Something to Admit—that I had sinned and was cut off from God (Rom 3:23; 6:23).
2. Something to Believe—that Jesus died in my place to take the punishment for my sin (Is 53:6).
3. Something to do—Come to him (Rev 3:20).

It has certain weaknesses. It does not emphasize man's rebellion, or the lordship of Christ. In the context, Jesus' words in Revelation 3:20 are not addressed to the unconverted individual. Nor does this outline highlight the cost of becoming a Christian. But it is very simple and very brief. It is easily remembered and can be clearly explained. The three steps can be turned into a short prayer around the familiar phrases—*Sorry* (that I am a sinner), *Thank you* (that Jesus died for me), *Please* (come into my heart).

Many youth leaders have used that outline, or a similar one, to the eternal benefit of many young people. In chapter four I wrote about the idea of a 'four year conversion' in youth work. The teaching programme of a youth fellowship should take that into account. As well as explaining the gospel person-to-person with his young people, a youth leader should have a Bible teaching programme that covers basic Christian ideas over an extended period. To work through the gospel of Mark, for example, on a regular basis with young people, will mean that they are called to a decision about Jesus Christ. The teaching programme and personal counselling will go hand-in-hand.

Another area of Christian teaching that is central to youth work is the doctrine of assurance. Young people who are converted need to have a clear answer to the questions, 'How can I be sure I am a Christian?' and, 'What happens if I sin?' They need to know that their salvation does not depend on their feelings, that it is not linked to how committed or enthusiastic they are, and that it is not arrogant for them to be certain. The answer to doubt is not greater excitement or deeper devotion, but a clearer knowledge of facts.

Teaching Christian assurance will involve teaching the

authority and the inspiration of the Bible. That may be the point at which a young person's faith is most directly assaulted in the classroom.

The Creator God

The implications of the doctrine of creation are also important for young people. Coming to terms with their own physical appearance and their character and abilities, understanding their sexuality, developing a Christian attitude to work and unemployment, responding to social and environmental issues, will all depend on the extent to which they realize that this world and every human being were created by God and rightly belong to him. The youth leader will need to work these out in detail with her young people, tailoring the applications of the teaching to their particular circumstances.[99]

I have not dealt in earlier chapters with involving young people in service for the community, but that would be one inevitable application of Bible teaching about the creation. If God is involved with the world he made, then his people must involve themselves with it too. If he longed to gather people under his wings (Lk 13:34), then his children must also reach out to them in love. Social involvement and evangelism should both spring out of good Bible teaching. They will both be on shaky foundations unless the young people first understand why they are doing them. We have sometimes been better at telling young people to get involved in social issues and in evangelism than we have been at teaching them why they should do so.

Earlier chapters have concentrated on the church and the family. They will both be important topics for teaching in Christian youth work. I have also touched at various points on the rampant materialism of Western society. Young people will never cope with the pressures to acquire more and more possessions and to seek an ever higher standard of living unless they are clearly taught the doctrine of stewardship. When they realize that nothing we ever have belongs to us, then they will be able to get their possessions into a right perspective.

They will need to be taught the biblical basis for Christian behaviour. The emphasis must fall on the cultivation of a Christian mind, not the imposition of a Christian behaviour pattern. Young people need to learn *how* to think about ethical problems, more than *what* to think about them.

Although I have been referring frequently in these paragraphs to teaching doctrine, please remember that the process of communicating these priceless spiritual truths is far more total than simple academic teaching on a classroom or seminar model. First the youth leader himself must understand and live out these truths. Sometimes our greatest need in youth work is not to teach truth better, but to understand it better. Then we must obey it fully. Then we *will* communicate it to our young people through our lives and our lips, even though we may feel incompetent as teachers in an academic sense.

At the same time, we need to remember that young people have a mental ability to grasp and remember new facts which they will not have when they are older. It is a good time for learning. In particular they will never find it easier to learn verses than when they are young. The learning of Bible verses should be a regular part of every youth group's life (Ps 119:9-11).

Through all teaching in youth ministry, the gospel will be central. It is the core of youth evangelism and the core of youth discipling. It is not something we ever get beyond in the Christian life.

Counselling

Counselling is another aspect of youth work that has the gospel at its heart.

I have suggested that the most effective part of our work

with young people will be where we focus our attention deeply on a few. Here we will build deep and lasting friendships which God's Spirit can use to build up both them and us. There will need to be a determination to persevere in offering friendship, even when a young person goes through an antagonistic stage and spurns that friendship. There will have to be restraint, so that no unfair moral pressure is put on the young person. There will have to be maturity, so that the leader can accept rejection and can allow the young person freedom and dignity to choose his or her own path.

There will also have to be sensitivity to the traumas and pains of adolescence. We will need to be aware of all the emotional undercurrents which run around a teenage peer group, and which sometimes make the social times the most painful parts of youth group life. The good youth leader watches the socio-dynamics of the youth group and tries to look beneath the surface of what is happening. He tries to be aware of the pain and the hurt, and to feel the pressures that his young people are feeling as they search out their own identities.

Skill in relating at this personal level can be improved when a team of leaders help one another by praying together and discussing their young people's needs. The value of a regular meeting of the youth leadership team will have become obvious much earlier in this book, but one of the most useful things to do at a team meeting is to analyse the group. The leader can circulate a list of the main members of the group and ask the other leaders to write down where they think each member of the group is at the moment, what they think that member's main spiritual needs are, and how they think the group could meet those needs.

Discussing each leader's insights into the individuals in the group can be a helpful exercise for the team (even if the team is only two leaders strong). Discussing how the group pro- gramme can meet those needs may be more profitable still. It may even revolutionize what you are doing. It will certainly lead to a recognition that many of the members' needs can be met only at a personal level.

The leadership team will be able to detect the spiritual links that God is building between particular leaders and particular members. It will be able to check those relationships when they become unhelpful. With adolescents it is inadvisable for male leaders to develop a counselling relationship with girl members, or female leaders with boy members.

A youth leadership team must always be aware of the dangers in this. When an element of sexual infatuation creeps into a counselling relationship, it will prove to be spiritually damaging in the long run. Firm or, if need be, drastic measures should be taken quickly. The advice and intervention of other leaders will be indispensable. The simple expedient of passing individual members of the group on to a leader of the same sex for counselling is a basic rule of youth work. So, for example, the 'sole' male leader of a group made up largely of older teenage girls *must* look urgently for a female colleague.

Secular or Christian counselling courses and anything written about adolescent psychology may be helpful (although they will have a tendency to be problem-orientated). The youth leader must develop the skill to feed the spiritual life of the ordinary young person, and not assume that Christian counselling is limited to helping those with problems. But it is certainly helpful to study the various counselling techniques: listening, evaluating, interpreting, probing, questioning, teaching, confronting, self-disclosing, encouraging, reflecting, and using silence (where some of the most significant, life-changing insights often come).

Whatever assistance we find to help us to do it, we must develop the ability to speak one-to-one about spiritual things. For most young people their deepest needs will not be met until someone sits down alongside them and applies Christ's teaching personally to them. Many Christians can tell how they were involved in a Christian community for some time, without being converted, but when someone spoke to them personally about their relationship with God, they came face to face with Jesus Christ and surrendered their lives to him. We all have a great ability to apply what we hear to everyone else rather than to ourselves. It is only when someone says, in effect, 'Thou art the man,' that we are forced to face the truth.

We retain the ability to avoid personal application even after conversion. Throughout our Christian lives we need those who will lovingly confront us with the truth about ourselves. The gospel is the heart of this ministry, for the unconverted and for the converted.

It may sometimes be too soon to go over a simple gospel outline (like the three steps on page 226) with someone, but it is never too late. It is not helpful to impose a detailed explanation of how to become a Christian on a spiritually indifferent young person. Until God's Spirit starts to work on his heart, the gospel will be like a pearl to a pig (Mt 7:6), but the converted young person never tires of hearing the gospel and needs to apply its truth to his life constantly.

The whole of the Christian life is about getting rid of sin.[100] The unconverted person has to repent, but so does the converted person; and to keep on repenting. In the letters to the seven churches in the book of Revelation, many of the Christians addressed must have had fine records of Christian service, but those who had lost their first love were not told to pray more, or to fast, or to seek for some wonderful new experience. The Lord told them to repent. Those who were compromising were not told to pray all night for revival. They were told to repent. The lukewarm Laodiceans were not told to serve more zealously. They were told to repent (see Rev 2 and 3).

We never leave the foot of the cross in the Christian life. Those who call this emphasis pietistic and turn young people's attention instead to the huge social and political problems of our world, condemn them to addressing that agenda out of guilt, and not out of gratitude.

We do not try to change our world because it needs changing and because, if we work hard enough, our efforts are going to make a difference to it. We try to change it because it is God's world and it is his purpose that it should be redeemed. He has made us part of that purpose by forgiving us for our sins and putting his Spirit into our hearts. It is our gratitude for what he has done for us that equips us to set about the agenda of social, political, economic, moral, legal and environmental issues that face us in our society today.

The tasks before the church are indeed huge, and young people must tackle them, but they will only find the strength for that work when their hearts are full of thanks to God because their sins have been put away, and forgiveness is their daily experience.

Grace is the heart of Christian theology and gratitude the heart of Christian ethics. In youth work, if we remove grace from our theology, guilt rather than gratitude will become the main motivating force for Christian behaviour. Guilt saps young people's strength. Gratitude frees them for service.

Christian youth counselling focuses on bringing to young people the news that God loves them, that he will forgive them because Jesus died in their place, and that his Spirit wants to take control of their lives to make his kingdom an increasing reality in this present age.

Finale

This is an appropriate note on which to bring this book to a close. There have been points at which I have felt the need to try to correct some current youth work practice, because it has seemed to me that it is not taking the Bible seriously. Lip service is paid to the authority of the Bible, but the sufficiency of the Bible to guide and direct youth work is not acknowledged in practice.

In trying to correct this, I may have failed to stress the excitement of working with young people. It is always exhilarating to serve Jesus Christ, but to be called to work among young people is particularly thrilling.

The furious pace of change in our society means that today's young people will grow up into a very different world. None of us know quite what that world will be like, or quite what challenges will face the church of the future, but equipping young people for that future is one of the most worthwhile tasks in Christian ministry.

A new generation of Christians who grow up knowing the Bible and loving the Lord Jesus has huge potential. Failings that we have come to take for granted, like the middle-class bias of the church, may be overturned in a generation. There may be a future Christian leader in your youth group at this moment, who will affect the national life of our country as much as John Wesley did.

The challenge for youth workers is to do God's work in God's way. Right practice will require right theology. The search for a correct theology will take us back to the Bible. We must read it humbly and expectantly, and we must keep reviewing our youth work in the light of what we find in its pages.

We must let it set our priorities. If I would emphasize any of the points I have been making, it is that the main strategic error in youth work is to ignore Christ's command to feed sheep. We concentrate too much energy on reaching outsiders through the programme and activities we offer. Spiritual impact does not come through the club premises, youth activities, events, or meetings. It comes in and through people. The most effective way outsiders are reached and drawn into the kingdom is by loving contact with those inside the kingdom. Fringe young people are drawn into Christianity by their contact with Christian young people.

So the quality of the spiritual lives of the Christian young people is the primary concern of the youth leader because they are the 'leaders' (in a biblical sense) much more than he is. Their leadership is a commitment to people, which is far more important than participating in decision-making or sharing organizational control.

The organization of youth work should not focus on programmes to present certain ideas to outsiders, but on building up young Christians to proclaim the gospel and to display the kingdom of God in practice. It is not primarily a quest for ideas that brings young people to Christ, but the quest for an authentic life-style. They can grasp this most easily when it is communicated through their own age group.

As Jesus lived alongside those he ministered to, and as Paul wrote 'we were ready to share with you not only the gospel of God but also our own selves' (1 Thess 2:8), so the youth worker must open his life to young people. Life-to-life communication is essential in youth work, but it will mean that we cannot minister effectively to very many people.

If the main strategic error in youth work is to ignore Christ's command to feed sheep, the main tactical error is to go for quantity rather than quality. We try to influence too many people at too shallow a level, instead of being prepared to build up a few into really authentic discipleship.

I end with this, because I once discovered how relevant it is to youth workers today. At a large national conference of Christian leaders, I asked a group of 150 youth workers (from a variety of backgrounds—'open' and 'church-based', inner-city, suburban and rural) to write down the names of the two or three young people they were influencing most deeply at that time in their ministries—the ones who ten years later would be significantly different because of their contact with the youth leader.

In the pause that followed I realized that I had touched base. Some were writing busily, but others were sitting with an expression on their faces which indicated that this question had never crossed their minds before; and now that it had, they couldn't answer it. They should have been able to. And so should you and I.

Notes

1. The nightlife is just a symptom, the outer and visible froth, of an inner, far deeper turbulence that boiled up in Britain around—if we must date it—1958, although some say as late as 1960. In that period youth captured this ancient island and took command in a country where youth has always before been kept properly in its place. Suddenly, the young own the town. (Article in *Weekend Telegraph*, 30 April 1965.)

2. In 1959 there were five million unmarried young people between fifteen and twenty-five years old. Their total uncommitted spending power was about £830 million. This represented only slightly over 5% of the national total consumer expenditure—a modest ratio for a group of people who constituted 13% of the population over fifteen. But it was a new feature of the market place (the real earnings of teenagers had increased by 50% between 1938 and 1958, much faster than those of adults), *and* it was available to go where the advertisers could lure it: nearly 20% went on clothing, 17% on drink and tobacco, 15% on coffee bars,

cafes and snacks, and a good share of the balance on 'entertainment goods'.

3. A survey of young people's views was commissioned by the Review Group on the Youth Service (which published the Thompson Report, *Experience and Participation*, in 1982 after the riots of the summer of 1981). This survey was published in 1983 as *Young People in the 80s*. Among its findings was this: 'Employment was the most important symbol signalling entrance into the adult world and was therefore a goal all were striving towards' (p. 27); 'Employment was a definite goal for all young people, since it was perceived to be the main route into the adult world, i.e. it conferred adult status. . . . Unemployment therefore robbed the individual of the opportunity to cross the symbolic and literal boundary between adolescence and adulthood, causing great anxiety and frustration' (p. 15).

4. Another finding of *Young People in the 80s* was this:

> The main goal of all the young people between the ages of fourteen to nineteen years was to reach adulthood—to be accepted by the adult world as 'grown up'. . . . Most found it extremely difficult to envisage or comprehend completion of the stages en route to full adulthood: 'It's not something you think about—I just want to grow up' (p. 21).

5. I am indebted for the next few paragraphs to Peter Cotterell's book, *Look Who's Talking!* (Kingsway, 1984) pp. 112f.

6. > Adolescents are excessively egoistic, regarding themselves as the centre of the universe and the sole object of interest, and yet at no time in later life are they capable of so much self-sacrifice and devotion. They form the most passionate love-relations, only to break them off as abruptly as they began them. On the one hand they throw themselves enthusiastically into the life of the community, and, on the other, they have an overpowering longing for solitude. They oscillate between blind submission to some self-chosen leader and defiant rebellion against any and every authority. They are selfish and materially-minded, and at the same time full of lofty idealism. They are ascetic, but will suddenly plunge into instinctive in-

dulgence of the most primitive character. At times their behaviour to other people is rough and inconsiderate, yet they themselves are extremely touchy. Their moods veer between lighthearted optimism and the blackest pessimism. Sometimes they will work with indefatigible enthusiasm, and at other times they are sluggish and apathetic (*The Ego and The Mechanism of Defence, 1937*).

The adolescent manifestations come close to symptom formation of the neurotic, psychotic or dissocial order and merge almost imperceptibly into . . . almost all the mental illnesses (*Psychoanalytic Study of the Child*).

It would be fair to say that the Freudians were describing middle-class, intelligent and articulate adolescents rather than their socially and culturally deprived, inner-city counterparts. The latter did not present themselves to the Anna Freud clinic in Hampstead or to her father's consulting room in Vienna.

7. John C. Coleman (in *The Nature of Adolescence*, Methuen, 1980) suggested that the two most influential theoretical approaches to adolescence, the psychoanalytical and the sociological, both 'view the teenage years as a "problem stage" in human development and . . . there is, as yet, no theoretical approach which embodies as its main tenet the essential normality of the adolescent process'.

There is, however, plenty of empirical work which challenges some of the presuppositions about teenage psychology. The survey of *Young People in the 80s* found that 'Parents were a primary source of advice about personal as well as more general problems, especially in relation to employment, but they also provided models for the young in respect of adulthood and adult responsibilities' (p. 13).

8. The contradiction between teachers' views of adolescence and what adolescents are really like emerges only too clearly from the results of two recent surveys. In one of them 80% of American high-school teachers questioned stated their conviction that adolescence is a time of great emotional disturbance. In the other, some 60% of a large sample of 14 to 15 year-olds

denied that they ever felt very miserable or depressed *(Seven Ages)*.

9. In 'I like to say . . . what I think' (*A Study of the Attitudes, Values and Beliefs of Young People Today*, 1984), Simmons and Wade state in their conclusions:

> It is our belief that the core values of the young are unlikely to differ greatly from those of the rest of society . . . the continuity of values between the generations has been greatly under-estimated. Undue attention has been drawn to those aspects of life, often colourful and occasionally bizarre, where parents and their young disagree . . .
>
> There seems to be no influential theory of normal adolescence. In the absence of such a theory a number of pervasive and enduring myths have grown up. These myths emphasise abnormality rather than normality in the young. Thus storm and stress, which may be experienced in some form by adults at any age, is portrayed as a necessary experience for *all* teenagers . . . to add insult to injury, young people who do not conform to the current mythology run the risk of being regarded as abnormal whereas those members of the older generation who sustain and nurture the prevailing myths frequently escape criticism by reason of their more advanced age and superior status (p. 212).

John C. Coleman in his study of adolescence came to very similar conclusions:

> There is no evidence to show that any but a small minority experience a serious identity crisis. In most cases relationships with parents are positive and constructive, and young people, by and large, do not reject adult values in favour of those espoused by the peer group. In fact, in most situations peer group values appear to be consistent with those of important adults, rather than in conflict with them. Fears of promiscuity among the young are not born out by the research findings, nor do studies support the belief that the peer group encourages anti-social behaviour, unless other factors are also present (*The Nature of Adolescence,* Methuen, 1980 p. 178).

10. From the point of view of our psychological development, starting a career can have enormous implications. It offers a solution to the identity crisis of adolescence by finally pro-

viding an answer to the question, Who (and what) am I? An adolescent may not like his or her first job, and may even be determined to quit it as soon as anything better turns up, but few would deny that they find it more reassuring to be able to say I am a secretary, salesman, or whatever, rather than I'm at school. Throughout our adult lives we use our jobs in this way to bolster up our self-image and to explain ourselves to other people. It is a major psychological bonus for working. . . . This aspect of work gives an even blacker hue to the already dark cloud of youth unemployment, because it implies that school-leavers who cannot get jobs may not only lose confidence in themselves but also fail to mature psychologically since they are deprived of a prop essential for normal development.

Boys are probably more at risk than girls in this respect, not only because work plays a more central role in men's lives but as another consequence of the fact that girls seem to be more mature than boys throughout the entire process of growing up . . . unemployment is a much greater psychological threat to men than it is to women (John Nicholson, op. cit. p. 94).

11. There are no social life-worlds specifically adapted to the unemployed condition (Tom Kitwood, op. cit. p. 239).

12. We are presenting the next generation with a world in which the raison d'être of our own generation—paid employment—is crumbling (Anne Sofer, *The Times*, 18 July 1983).

13. In a study of the attitudes of sixteen to twenty-five year olds (*Young and Unemployed,* Costello, 1985), Dr Leslie Francis found that young people who had experienced some unemployment during the past two years generally were more depressed. They reported more signs of loneliness, anxiety, worry, isolation, self-doubt, despondency and dependency. They were also more radical. They were more likely to reject the moral values society traditionally imposes on issues like abortion, divorce, sexuality and the use of drugs. But, while rejecting the social and public side of religion, they professed a greater dependence upon the personal and private practice of religion (29% of those with no experience of unemployment had prayed during

the last week, but 39% of the long-term unemployed claimed to have done so).

14.   . . . the young are very realistically prepared for the uncertainties of the future, and although the Government would not admit it, special measures for tackling youth unemployment amount to a preparation for living with sub-employment, getting rid of unrealistic expectations, and reinforcing the coping mechanisms that the young have found for themselves (*Youthaid* Bulletin No. 6, as summarized in *Frontier Youth Trust* information service update).

15. See *Shadows of Adolescence* by Allan Kennedy (National Youth Bureau, 1984), for a picture of the problems facing young people in West Dorset.

16.   The cultural and class captivity of our churches is glaringly reflected in their work with young people (Michael Eastman, *Third Way,* February 1985).

17. *Where the Wastelands End* (Faber & Faber, 1973) p. 441 f.

18. See the report in the Home Office *Research and Planning Unit Bulletin,* July 1985.

19. Certain questions have been raised about the methodology of this enquiry and its conclusions may not be completely authoritative.

20. When he was a youth worker at the Mayflower Centre, Pip Wilson wrote about the exploitation of video in the inner-city:

> Video is the new urban toy. In Canning Town so many families have videos at £1 a night from the legal shops, 75p a night from the Chinese Take-Away—or the lowest I have heard of—40p a night from the Off Licence.
>
> Loveless sex, extreme violence, are the ones the kids talk about and parents, it seems to me, are allowing more and more of this influence into their homes. Sexual love is being replaced by the social norm of sex for one's gratification. What does this do for a child's future relationships?
>
> The *Sunday Times* has picked up the video influence and says of the *Driller Thriller,* 'which shows a man screaming while an electric drill is driven through his forehead . . .', or *Nightmares in a Damaged Brain* 'A ten year old hacks off a

woman's head with an axe, as she is having sexual intercourse with his father' *(Mayflower Youth Work Report 36)*.

21. The most highly-paid writers, actors, musicians, and producers in the world are not those that create education for the young, or drama for adults, or political programmes for others. They are the men and women who create television commercials (Ben H. Bagdikian, *The Information Machines: Their Impact on Men and The Media*).

22. For so long as young people feel repressed and awkward, as long as society can indulge one affluent and self-centred generation after another, as long as there is electricity, there will be rock music (S. Lawhead, *Rock Reconsidered*).

23. Much unhappiness can arise when the child's expectations about marriage are conditioned by one culture (Western) and the parents' expectations by another (Eastern).

24. For example, social interaction is the most important single factor in their choice of leisure activities (see *Young People in the 80s,* p. 44).

25. James Fowler notes that the most common structure of faith found in adolescents 'is conformist in nature in that it is highly aware of the opinions, expectations and judgments of significant others. Adolescents do not yet have a sufficiently formulated identity to have autonomous beliefs, evaluations and perceptions' (*Stages of Faith,* Harper & Row, 1981).

26. The apostle Paul *may* be referring to such a period of innocence in the middle of his complicated argument in Romans: 'I was once alive apart from the law, but when the commandment came, sin revived and I died' (Rom 7:9). In one sense Paul had never been 'apart from the law' ('circumcized on the eighth day, of the people of Israel, of the tribe of Benjamin, a Hebrew born of Hebrews . . .' Phil 3:5), but there was a period of his life when he was not separated from God by his conscious disobedience to the commandments. It is not clear whether that period was only during his earliest infancy, or whether it extended to the ceremony at which he

became a 'son of the commandment', i.e. assumed personal responsibility to keep the law.

27. 1 Corinthians 13:11 does not invalidate this. Paul there implies that the child has an immature understanding of God, but not an immature (or deficient) relationship with him.

28. Particularly now youth unemployment is increasingly postponing for a great many their entry into the adult world indefinitely. (See pages 18, 19, 23–27).

29. There is also Elihu. I am never certain whether the reader is meant to approve of his contribution or not but, as the fourth of Job's comforters, he withheld his speech until the end because the other three and Job himself were much older than he (Job 32:4-10). So he also may be an example of commendable endeavour by the young.

30. Our task with this world is not to explain it, but convert it. Its need can be met, not by the discovery of its own immanent principle in signal manifestation through Jesus Christ, but only by the shattering impact on its self-sufficiency and arrogance of the Son of God, crucified, risen and ascended, pouring forth that holy and disruptive energy which is the Holy Ghost (William Temple, 1939).

31. In contradicting the emphasis of the Board of Education report, I must not give the impression that God does not have a very individual purpose for which he created each one of us. He certainly does, and by redemption and the work of the Spirit, we begin to become what he always intended us to be. This aspect of the report is right.

Jesus valued and welcomed individuals. He dealt with almost everyone differently, *but,* in an appropriate way, he challenged each person to repent of sin and to accept his lordship.

32. Of course, the cross is not the whole of the gospel! The resurrection and the Spirit, indeed the whole life of Jesus (majoring on the cross and resurrection), were at the heart of the kerygma (see the analysis of the evangelistic

sermons in Michael Green's *Evangelism in the Early Church,* Hodder & Stoughton, 1970).

The first Christians did highlight different aspects of this kerygma for different audiences—e.g. (i) Acts 17 where intelligent Greek pagans get a dose of God as immanent, though inevitably Paul gets round to judgement and resurrection (but there is nothing on the life of Jesus, or Jesus as Messiah, and not much on the cross); (ii) When faced with Gentile audiences, 'Jesus is Lord' is more the message than 'Jesus is the Christ (Messiah)'. There were limits to this variation, but the variation existed (hence the theological debate on the different New Testament christologies).

For us now, the point is that we can and must vary our presentation of the unchanging gospel to meet the cultural situation of our age. *But* there are essentials that cannot be omitted and there are many cultural accretions that need challenging. The gospel can be presented in many ways and with varying emphases, as long as the variation falls within New Testament limits.

(I am indebted to Christopher Byworth for suggesting this clarification and qualification of the text at this point.)

33. For a discussion of the place of the big event in youth ministry see chapter seven (pp. 158–162).

34. *Flirting with the World* (Hodder & Stoughton, 1982) pp. 128-9.

35. Tom Kitwood provides powerful corroboration of this point:

> Out of a total of seventy-four categorized choices there were only eleven cases of a boy or girl 'standing alone' for a value at the level of action . . ., nine of which came from those who were over seventeen years old. . . . The probable inference is that standing alone in this way is indeed rare, and almost unknown in the younger age-group. . . . The opinion of the boy who took part was that it was inconceivable for a person below the age of about sixteen to hold values in an individual way. Boys and girls below that age did, of course, have

values, but these arose from participation in group activity (*Disclosures to a Stranger,* p. 165).

36. See J.I. Packer, *Knowing God* (Hodder & Stoughton, 1973) p. 124.

37. H.C.G. Moule, *The Second Epistle to Timothy: The Devotional Commentary Series* (Religious Tract Society, 1905) p. 16.

38. *Disclosures to a Stranger* p. 260.

39. Paul clearly believed that the message he preached must control the methods he used to proclaim it (2 Cor 4:1-5). He had to preach Jesus, not himself, but his life was to 'serve' the ministry of the gospel to his hearers (see verse 5).

    The priority of the message itself is even clearer when Paul wrote about those who preached the gospel from mixed motives:

    > Some indeed preach Christ from envy and rivalry, but others from good will. The latter do it out of love, knowing that I am put here for the defence of the gospel; the former proclaim Christ out of partisanship, not sincerely but thinking to afflict me in my imprisonment. What then? Only that in every way, whether in pretence or in truth, Christ is proclaimed; and in that I rejoice (Phil 1:15-18).

    It is striking that Paul rejoiced even when Christ was proclaimed 'in pretence'. He knew that the message of Christ had its own power to bring life to the hearers, quite independent of the sincerity of the motives or the integrity of the lives of those who proclaimed it. We need to have the same confidence.

40. Lawrence O. Richards, *Youth Ministry* (Zondervan, 1972) p. 128.

41. John Benington, *Culture, Class and Christian Beliefs* (Scripture Union, 1973) p. 64.

42. As a comment on Gavin Reid's survey, it should be pointed out that most people are unable to specify exactly what led to their conversion. It is usually a combination of

factors and a survey of this sort should not cause us to abandon certain forms of evangelism. Rather we should be encouraged to use every means at our disposal to face people with the claims of Christ, especially those means with a personal dimension to them (1 Cor 9:19-23).

43. D.C.K. Watson, *You Are My God* (Hodder & Stoughton, 1983) p. 39.

44. Richards comments, 'Christian education of youth which fails to build towards a strong Christian peer group will never achieve maximum impact' (*Youth Ministry*).

45. Richards, ibid., p. 152.

46. See the *Serendipity* material published by Scripture Union.

47. 'No man in all history has succeeded in making men more holy, more Christlike than he was himself' (Michael Saward & Michael Eastman, *Christian Youth Group*, Scripture Union, 1965), although we need to remember that *we* do not make men holy. God does, and with the influence of others, he may cause our protégés to overtake us in the spiritual life.

48. See page 79.

49. While the Bible presents a strong framework for family life, no hierarchy is imposed within it. There is no teaching that, for example, grandparents are very important and grandchildren are less important. But well-ordered family life is important, and it does require leadership within the family (see chapter eight). Paul's emphasis in the Pastoral epistles on the well-managed family (1 Tim 5:8) showed the same concern for lifemodels of the faith that was present in the passages of the law we have already considered (e.g. Deut 6:4-9).

> A bishop [or elder] must be above reproach, the husband of one wife, temperate, sensible, dignified, hospitable. . . . He must manage his own household well, keeping his children submissive and respectful in every way; for if a man does not know how to manage his own household, how can he care for

God's church? (1 Tim 3:2-5).

The family was a microcosm of the church. In the family the young learned to grow up physically and temperamentally by living alongside those older than themselves. So in the church there must be life-models of mature faith which encourage other members to maturity. The bishop (or elder) had to communicate the faith life-to-life, so that all could mature together.

50. 'Youthtrack', *The Harvester*, 1985.
51. *The Christian Youth Group* (Scripture Union, 1965).
52. Quoted in Bernard Levin, *The Pendulum Years* (Pan, 1970) p. 91.
53. Quoted in *Little Fat Buzz* (Hodder & Stoughton, 1977).
54. See Dr Leslie J. Francis, *Teenagers and The Church* (Collins, 1984).
55. Ibid.
56. Clifford Longley in *The Times*, 30 April 1984.
57. 'Participation', resource paper in CYFA Leaders' *Training and Resource Manual* (CYFA, 1984).
58. Michael Griffiths, *Cinderella With Amnesia* (IVP, 1975) p. 103.
59. Ibid. pp. 104-107.
60. John Briggs, *Christian Graduate*, September 1978.
61. Michael Griffiths op. cit. p. 106.
62. Michael Griffiths op. cit. p. 106-107.
63. There is at least one more biblical mark of the local church, not mentioned by Michael Griffiths, which is the 'all in each place' principle (1 Cor 1:2). The New Testament does not envisage rival Christian groups living close to one another and yet not meeting or knowing each other.

   As numbers grew in cities like Corinth, with no special buildings, Christians would have had to meet in different homes (hence, perhaps, the 'I belong to Apollos' of 1 Corinthians 3:4?), but they were all expected to come together for the Lord's Supper (1 Cor 11:8—'when you assemble as a church') and Paul criticizes them for not acting in love and discerning the body when they do.

This emphasis is relevant in youth work because young people can rarely make sense of denominational divisions. They feel a strong loyalty to other young Christians in their own area and appreciate opportunities to meet up with them (see p. 159 f. and pp. 218–220).

64. Quoted by Michael Eastman in *Inside Out* (Falcon, 1976) p. 124.

65. New Testament Theology (IVP, 1981) p. 788.

66. *The Temporary Community—Organised Camping for Urban Society* (Albatross, 1984) p. 195.

67. John Stott, *Issues Facing Christians Today* (Marshalls, 1984) p. 209.

68. *Counselling Teenagers* (Group Books, 1984) p. 514.

69. *The Call to Conversion* (Lion, 1982) p. 119.

70. *A Long Way From Home* (Paternoster Press, 1979) pp. 50, 53.

71. *Parents and Teenagers* (Victor Books, 1984) p. 328.

72. *Hide or Seek* (Hodder & Stoughton, 1982) p. 119, quoting Marguerite and Willard Beecher: *Parents on the Run*.

73. In their own way, parents, too, may face an 'identity crisis'. The parent of the average adolescent is entering middle age. At a time when their children are approaching the peak of their physical and sexual vigour, parents are faced with the fact that they have passed their own physical peaks, and that the rest of the road slopes downhill, however gently at first. In a society as obsessed with youth as our own—and as scornful of old age—the prospect can sometimes be a painful one (John Conger, *Adolescence—Generation Under Pressure*, Harper & Row, 1979, p. 38).

74. See *Hide or Seek* p. 53.

75. *Parents in Pain* (IVP, 1979) p. 207.

76. *Hide or Seek* p. 23.

77. *Hide or Seek* p. 159.

78. Peter Dawson, *The Times,* 28 October 1974.

79. *Proverbs* (IVP, 1964) p. 147.

80. *Young People in the Eighties* (HMSO, 1983) pp. 47, 50.
81. See Kitwood op. cit. p. 226f.
82. *Adolescents and Society*. The Arthur Mellows Memorial Lecture, 1962.
83. Kitwood op. cit. p. 253.
84. Barry St Clair in *Parents and Teenagers* (Victor Books, 1984) p. 628.
85. James Dobson, *Preparing for Adolescence* (Kingsway Publications, 1982) pp. 41-44.
86. Larry Richards in *Parents and Teenagers* p. 636.
87. Helen Lee, *The Troubled Years* (Falcon Books, 1968) p. 55.
88. Keith Olson, *Counselling Teenagers* (Group Books, 1984) p. 514.
89. The question of Paul's strategy and guidance is more complicated than it might appear. At times he appeared to adapt his strategy almost day by day in response to God's leading:

> And they went through the region of Phrygia and Galatia, having been forbidden by the Holy Spirit to speak the word in Asia. And when they had come opposite Mysia, they attempted to go into Bithynia, but the Spirit of Jesus did not allow them; so, passing by Mysia, they went down to Troas. And a vision appeared to Paul in the night: a man of Macedonia was standing beseeching him and saying, 'Come over to Macedonia and help us.' And when he had seen the vision, immediately we sought to go on into Macedonia, concluding that God had called us to preach the gospel to them (Acts 16:6-10).

But on other occasions he maintained his strategic purpose even in the face of apparently divine guidance not to: 'Through the Spirit they told Paul not to go on to Jerusalem' (Acts 21:5, see also Acts 21:10-14).
90. We can find New Testament justification for the drawing of boundaries in the agreement that Paul should go to the uncircumcized and Peter to the circumcized (Gal 2:7), and in the appointment of the first 'deacons' (Acts 6:1-6). It is

also implicit in the listing of specific spiritual gifts (Rom 12:6-8, etc).

91. It is not easy to justify a limited contract period directly from the Bible, but it is clear that an individual's sphere of ministry can and should change—like Moses after receiving the advice of his father-in-law (Exod 18:13-27) and Paul after his imprisonment.

92. That this is a biblical principle can be seen from the corporate leadership that is normal in the New Testament (see chapter six, pp. 126). We also see Paul reporting to the council in Jerusalem (Acts 15), and keeping in touch with his mother-church at Antioch (Acts 13:1-3; 14:26-28; 15:30-35; 18:22). Paul made the point powerfully that his ultimate accountability was to God alone (1 Cor 4:1-6).

93. We have already considered the biblical grounds for this in examining the way Jesus worked with the apostles and the way Paul worked (in chapters five and six).

94. For the reasons mentioned in chapter six, pp. 111 f.

95. *I like to say what I think* p. 204.

96. *Seven Ages* p. 76.

97. Throughout the chapter I have had in mind the more common pattern of church-based youth work in the UK, which is that done by volunteers. There is a new and very welcome development of more local churches appointing full-time church-based youth workers. There are some clear differences about this sort of work (for example, a short contract period is not necessarily desirable for a full-time worker). We have much to learn from North America in this particular area.

98. Bob Moffett's *Crowdbreakers* (Pickering & Inglis, 1983) has a helpful short chapter on communication in the youth group (pp. 9-14), and an excellent compendium of games and activities which can be used to liven up teaching sessions on particular themes. Anton Baumohl's *Making Adult Disciples* (Scripture Union, 1984) is very helpful on all aspects of Christian education, particularly

activity-based learning.

99. One helpful book for the youth leader, although probably not for the young people, would be John Stott's *Issues Facing Christians Today* (Marshalls, 1984).

100. To state it in this way is not to deny the other side of the same truth: to be rid of sin we must be constantly filled with the Spirit. We are not to leave the house empty for 'seven other spirits more evil' than the first (Mt 12:43–45). We need the constant infilling and empowering of God's Spirit at every point in the Christian life.

Index of Resource Agencies

Probably your best resource point is the local Christian bookshop. There you should find the latest youth resources and probably a video library. A regular visit will be useful to the youth worker.

I have listed below some of the Christian organizations which specialize in different areas of youth work.

General resource agencies

British Youth for Christ (Schools, evangelism, unemployment projects)
Cleobury Place, Cleobury Mortimer, Kidderminster, Worcestershire DY14 8JG. Tel: 0299 270260.

Church Youth Fellowships Association (Leadership training and resource materials)
Falcon Court, 32 Fleet Street, London EC4Y 1DB. Tel: 01 353 0751.

Inter-Schools Christian Fellowship (Schools work of Scripture Union)
130 City Road, London EC1V 2NJ. Tel: 01 250 1966.

Pathfinders (Specialist in 11-14 age group)
Falcon Court, 32 Fleet Street, London EC4Y 1DB. Tel: 01 353 0751.

Scripture Union (Publishing, Bible-reading aids, missions, leadership training)
130 City Road, London EC1V 2NJ. Tel: 01 250 1966.

'Open' and 'detached' youth work

Frontier Youth Trust
130 City Road, London EC1V 2NJ. Tel: 01 250 1966.

Youth volunteer agency

Careforce
130 City Road, London EC1V 2NJ. Tel: 01 250 1966.

Youth movements

Campaigners
Campaigner House, St Mark's Close, Colney Heath, Hertfordshire AL4 0NQ. Tel: 0727 24065.

Covenanters
104 Bloom Street, Manchester M1 6HU. Tel: 061 236 2305.

Crusaders
Crusader House, 2 Romeland Hill, St Albans, Hertfordshire AL3 4ET. Tel: 0727 55422.

Evangelistic agencies

Down to Earth
201 Wickham Chase, West Wickham, Kent BR4 0BH.

Operation Mobilisation
The Quinta Christian Centre, Weston Rhym, Oswestry, Shropshire SY10 7LR. Tel: 0691 773388.

Saltmine Trust
PO Box 15, Dudley, West Midlands DY3 2AN. Tel: 0384 238224.

Youth With a Mission
Holmstead Manor, Staplefield Road, Cuckfield, West Sussex RH17 5JF. Tel: 0444 416961.

Students

Campus Crusade for Christ
103 Friar Street, Reading, Berkshire RG1 1EP. Tel: 0734 589461.

The Navigators
Tregaron House, 27 High Street, New Malden, Surrey KT3 4BY. Tel: 01 942 2211.

Universities and Colleges Christian Fellowship
38 De Montfort Street, Leicester LE1 7GP. Tel: 0533 551700.

Aid organizations

Christian Aid
PO Box No 1, London SW9 8BH. Tel: 01 733 5500.

TEAR Fund
100 Church Road, Teddington, Middlesex TW11 8QE. Tel: 01 977 9144.

Mission organizations

A number of the missionary societies have youth secretaries and produce materials suitable for youth groups. In particular:

Bible Churchmen's Missionary Society
251 Lewisham Way, London SE4 1XF. Tel: 01 691 6111.

Church Missionary Society
157 Waterloo Road, London SE1 8UU. Tel: 01 928 8681.

Overseas Missionary Fellowship
Belmont, The Vine, Sevenoaks, Kent TN13 3TZ. Tel: 0732 456810.

South American Missionary Society
Allen Gardiner House, Pembury Road, Tunbridge Wells, Kent TN2 3QU. Tel: 0892 38647/8.

Arts festivals

Crossfire '86
PO Box 15, Liverpool L27 7XZ. Tel: 051 487 0955.

Greenbelt Festivals
11 Uxbridge Street, London W8 7AT. Tel: 01 229 7231.

Bible resource agencies

Bible Society
Stonehill Green, Westlea, Swindon, Wiltshire SN5 7DG. Tel: 0793 486381.

Creative Publishing
6 Pembroke Road, Moor Park, Northwood, Middlesex HA6 2HR. Tel: 092 74 21412.

Scripture Union (Bible ministries)
130 City Road, London EC1V 2NJ. Tel: 01 250 1966.

Denominational organizations

Assemblies of God
106-114 Talbot Street, Nottingham NG1 5GH. Tel: 0602 474525.

Baptist Union of Great Britain and Ireland
Baptist Church House, 4 Southampton Row, London WC1B 4AB. Tel: 01 405 9803.

British Council of Churches
2 Eaton Gate, London SW1W 9BL. Tel: 01 730 9611.

General Synod Board of Education (Church of England)
Church House, Dean's Yard, London SW1P 3NZ. Tel: 01 222 9011.

Methodist Association of Youth Clubs
2 Chester House, Pages Lane, Muswell Hill, London N10 1PR. Tel: 01 444 9845.

United Reformed Church
86 Tavistock Place, London WC1H 9RT. Tel: 01 837 7661.